D0913808

Tales and Parables of Sri Ramakrishna

SRI RAMAKRISHNA MATH
MYLAPORE, CHENNAI 600 004

Published by
Adhyaksha
Sri Ramakrishna Math
Mylapore, Chennai-4

First Edition, August 1943
Second Edition, June 1947
Thirty-one Print, July 2015
2M3C

Total number of copies printed till now: 1,16,600

ISBN 81-7823-111-5

Printed in India at
Sri Ramakrishna Math Printing Press
Mylapore, Chennai-4

Once a man went to a certain place to see a theatrical performance, carrying a mat under his arm. Hearing that it would be some time before the performance began, he spread the mat on the floor and fell asleep. When he woke up all was over. Then he returned home with the mat under his arm!

—*Sri Ramakrishna*

Preface to the First Edition

The abstruse ideas of religion and philosophy have an unerring appeal when clothed in homely imagery. Great truths are easily comprehended when expressed through a simple figure or similitude. The homeliness of the outer crust endows the core of the teaching with an effortless familiarity, ensuring its usefulness in the day to day life of religious practice. Parables therefore occupy a most important place in the teachings of the saints and seers. Jesus and Muhammad, Buddha, and the Vedic Sages have again and again adopted the allegorical method of presentation as an effective way of religious instruction. In this respect they have widely differed from professional philosophers and theologians. The Bible tells us that when Jesus delivered one of his parables, 'the people were astonished at his doctrine, for he taught as one having authority and not as the scribes'. The directness of appeal inherent in parables is well borne out by this observation. Another point about the way in which the great Teachers taught deserves mention here. When Jesus taught the gathered crowd his first parable, he was questioned by his disciples as to the propriety of speaking to the multitude in parables. His reply was that by so doing he had thrown a veil over the inner import, making it difficult of comprehension by all except those who really cared to understand. This should not be taken as an indication of a narrow conservatism in his outlook; on the contrary, it points out only the excellence of the methodology adopted by true and great Teachers of men. Easy winning makes the prize always cheap. The *Mahabharata* hands down to us an ancient tradition which advises teachers to part with the great truths of religion only to earnest enquirers. The motive of Jesus was not different from this. Sri Ramakrishna, the spiritual teacher *par excellence* that he was, however, does not make any effort to make his parables obscure; the morals they convey lie on the surface. Many of his parables are drawn from ordinary domestic and social life, customary with the people who lived around him. Some he had devised on the model of Puranic stories. But all have a humorous vein and bear witness to his consummate wit and keenness of observation. We hope this collection of the parables published for the first time in separate book form will be of service to all who wish to get some acquaintance with the fundamentals of spiritual life through the interesting medium of parables and stories.

August, 1943 *Publisher*

Preface to the Second Edition

The present volume is an improvement, quite a large improvement, upon *The Parables of Sri Ramakrishna,* which was first published in August, 1943. It will be noticed that the name of the book has been changed a little. This change has been necessitated because of the incorporation of new matter in the book. Now, apart from an exhaustive collection of the parables of the Master, we have here a bumper harvest of his tales as well.

The addition of the tales has been thought needful because the distinction between a *tale* and a *parable*—as they are understood from the standpoint of a profound spiritual preceptor and an eager aspirant—is often insignificant. With them a *tale* becomes a *parable* as easily as a tadpole a frog. Secondly, the element of didacticism which makes the primary difference between a tale and a parable is equally pronounced in both the tales and parables of the Master. Again though generally the tales of the Master are based on facts of his own or others' experience in life, yet the strange eye with which they are seen and the mystic way they are narrated give them all a more or less parabolic stamp.

For the convenience of the readers, the tales and the parables have been brought under different groupings according to the spirit they strongly evince. But these groupings should not be taken as rigid and absolute, for like the facets of a gem, there are several aspects to a tale or parable of the Master.

To make the collection exhaustive we have freely used different books of the Ramakrishna-Vivekananda literature of which *The Gospel of Sri Ramakrishna* has supplied the main bulk. We have taken that version of a tale or a parable—for, several of them have more than one version (all of them authentic, being spoken by the Master in different contexts)—which is more pleasant and richer with story element.

We have also added in this edition an Introduction, which gives a short account of the life and teachings of Sri Ramakrishna.

We believe that this enlarged edition will be of greater use and benefit to all readers.

May, 1947 *Publisher*

Contents

THE BANE OF WORLDLINESS:

'KAMA-KANCHANA' (LUST AND GOLD):

MAYA:

PITFALLS:

EGOTISM: VANITY

BOOK III

BRAHMAN:

ASPECTS OF THE DIVINE:

MAN IN DIVINE STATE:

BOOK IV

COUNSELS:

TRUTHS PROFOUND:

Introduction

SRI RAMAKRISHNA

A Short Account of His Life and Teachings

On February 18, 1836, was born in India a man of God, who has come to be known as Sri Ramakrishna— a name which spontaneously evokes in the minds of millions of Hindus heart-full adoration and love. Above the din and confusion of modern life we hear the clarion call of Sri Ramakrishna directing our attention to the deeper verities of existence.

The life of Sri Ramakrishna, though devoid of spectacular events, is filled with spiritual romance of the rarest type. The fifty-one years of his mortal existence give us vivid stories of religion in practice. During these years he constantly lived on the exalted plane of God-consciousness. The natural tendency of his mind was to soar above the phenomena of the world. It seems to the reader of his biography that he brought down his mind with utmost difficulty to the ordinary level in order to talk with men and women. His sayings are not those of a learned man, but pages from the Book of Life, written with the fluid of his own experiences and realisations. His utterances have upon them the badge of authority.

Sri Ramakrishna was born of poor parents living in Kamarpukur, a wayside village of Bengal. His father was full of piety and never deviated from the path of truth. He was dispossessed of his ancestral house and property as he refused to bear false witness to the advantage of his landlord. He observed all the strict disciplines of the life of a Brahmin, devoting most of the time to prayers and meditation as enjoined by his religion. He was content to lead a life of utter simplicity, practically depending upon God for his daily food and other necessities of life. The mother was full of womanly grace and her heart overflowed with the sweet milk of kindness for her neighbours. Many a time she would turn over her own meal to the poor and needy and thus starve for the whole day. She was always respected by the villagers for the crystal sincerity of her character and the total absence of guile and other sordid traits of worldly nature. Sri Ramakrishna, like other lads of his age, was full of fun and life, mischievous and charming, with a feminine grace he preserved to the end of his life. He was adored and petted by the young girls and women of the village. They found in him a kindred and understanding spirit. It was a dream of his childhood, as he told later on, to be reborn as a little Brahmin widow, a lover of Krishna who would visit her in her house. Sri Ramakrishna showed, during the years of his childhood, a precocious understanding of the deeper mysteries of the spiritual realm. He manifested supreme indifference to the education imparted in the school. It did not proceed beyond the most rudimentary stage. He used to say, later on, that books are fetters which impede the free expression of the soul. But even at the early age he possessed great wisdom. One day during that period of his life, he gave in a learned assembly of the Pundits a simple solution to an intricate problem of theology which had been puzzling the brains of those astute book-worms. This profound wisdom uttered in simple words, and coming directly from his soul characterised all his later sayings. The soul is the fountain of all knowledge and wisdom, but in the commonalty it is covered by a thick pall of ignorance created by our so-called experiences of life. But simple and artless saints, like a Christ or a Ramakrishna, always have had access to this perennial fountain-head of knowledge. Sri Ramakrishna took special delight in studying and hearing about the great heroes and heroines of the Hindu religious epics. Stories of saints and association with them always set his imagination on fire and created an exalted state of mind. He often played truant from school. The simple village had an extensive mango grove where he would repair with his schoolmates and enact dramas, selecting episodes from the Ramayana and the Mahabharata. The boy, with his clear skin, beautiful flowing locks, charming voice and independent spirit, would always play the leading parts. He also showed efficiency in clay-modelling.

At the age of seven Sri Ramakrishna lost his father. This event, which cast a gloom over the whole family, made the boy more thoughtful and serious. Now and then he was found strolling alone in the mango grove or the cremation ground. His serious nature, though hidden under the thin film of boyish merriment, perhaps got a glimpse of the transitoriness of human life. After that he became more attached to his mother and every day spent some time with her assisting her in the household work and daily worship in the family chapel. He thought it his duty to lessen the burden of his mother's grief and to infuse into her melancholy life whatever joy and consolation he could. Instinctively he shrank from objects and ideas that might prove obstacles to his future spiritual progress. His first spiritual ecstasy was the outcome of his innate artistic nature. Observing the flight of a flock of cranes with their snow-white wings shining against the background of the sky covered with dark rain-clouds, he lost physical consciousness and said afterwards that he had felt, in that state, an ineffable peace. More than once, during the period of boyhood, he experienced the bliss of spiritual ecstasy evoked by the contemplation of divine ideas.

At the age of seventeen, Sri Ramakrishna came to Calcutta, then the metropolitan city of India, where his elder brother conducted a Sanskrit academy. To the earnest request of his brother to continue his studies in keeping with the tradition of the Brahminical ancestry, the boy made the spirited and significant reply, "Brother, what shall I do with a mere bread-winning education? I shall rather acquire that wisdom which will illumine my heart and in getting which one is satisfied forever." In his vivid imagination he saw the scholars of Calcutta, devoid of wisdom, scrambling for recognition and power. Regarding the merely intellectual Pundits, without a higher idealism, he would say, later on, "They are like vultures who soar high on the wings of their undisciplined intellect, having their attention fixed, all the time, on the carrion of name, fame and wealth."

The life of Sri Ramakrishna took a new turn when he was engaged as a priest in a temple where the Deity is worshipped as the Divine Mother of the Universe under the name of Kāli. Seated before the graceful basalt image, he would often ask himself, "Is this image filled with the indwelling presence of God? Or is it mere stone, devoid of life and spirit, worshipped by countless devotees from time immemorial?" Now and then a kind of scepticism would creep into his soul and fill his mind with intense agony. But his inborn intuition revealed to him the evanescent nature of the objects of sense-enjoyment and the presence of a deeper reality behind the phenomena. He conceived of God as our Eternal Mother who is ever ready to grant us the priceless boon of divine wisdom if we only turn our gaze from the shadowy objects of this world. For a few days he worshipped the Deity following the rituals and ceremonies of his ancestors. But his was a soul not to be satisfied with a mere mechanical observance of religion. He craved for the vision of God.

Soon, before the onrush of his fervour, formalities of religion were swept away. Henceforth his worship consisted of the passionate cry and prayer of a child pained at the separation from his beloved Mother. For hours he would sing the songs composed by seers of God. Tears, then, would flow continuously from his eyes. He would weep and pray, "O Mother! Where art Thou? Reveal Thyself to me. Many devotees before me obtained Thy grace. Am I a wretch that Thou dost not come to me? Pleasure, wealth, friends, enjoyments—I do not want any of these. I only desire to see Thee, Mother." He spent day and night in such agonising prayer. Words of a worldly nature would singe, as it were, his ears. Often people would be amazed to see him rolling on the ground and rubbing his face against the sand with the piteous wail, "Another day is spent in vain, Mother, for I have not seen Thee!

Another day of this short life has passed and I have not realised the Truth!" In another mood, he would sit before the Deity and say to Her, "Art Thou true, Mother, or is it all a fiction of the mind—mere poetry without any reality? If Thou dost exist, why can I not see Thee? Is religion then a phantasy, a mere castle in the air?" Scarcely would these words pass his lips when in a flash he would recollect the lives of saints who had actually seen God in this life. "She can't be a mere freak of human imagination," the young worshipper would think, "there are people who have actually seen Her. Then why can't I see Her? Life is passing away. One day is gone followed by another, never to return. Every day I am drawing much nearer to death. But where is my Mother? The scriptures say that there is only one thing to be sought in this life and that is God. Without Him life is unbearable, a mockery. When God is realised, life has a meaning, it is a pleasure, a veritable garden of ease. Therefore in pursuit of God sincere devotees renounce the world and sacrifice their lives.

What is this life worth if I am to drag on a miserable existence from day to day without tapping the eternal source of Immortality and Bliss?" Thoughts like these would only increase his longing and make him redouble his efforts to realise God. As a consequence he was blessed with the realisation of God. Regarding this God-vision he said, later on, to Swami Vivekananda, "Yes, my child, I have seen God, only more intensely than I see you. I have talked to God and more intensely than I am talking to you." Sri Ramakrishna used to emphasise that if an aspirant shows the same attachment to God as the miser feels for his hoarded treasure, the devoted wife for her beloved husband and the helpless child for its affectionate mother, God is sure to reveal Himself to such a fervent soul in three days.

A tremendous statement for these modern times. Yes, he has seen God! Not as an extracosmic Being, not as the personification of moral law, but as the very substratum of our being, the indwelling presence in all, in whom all human and moral relationships reach their culmination. His vision of God was not a remote entity of theology nor the vague dream of a poet, but the irresistible content of his inner experience. Is it not a great inspiration to know that a man of our own times could assert that he had seen God, when humanity as a whole seems to be moving away from the deeper aspect of life? The first impression even a casual reader of the life and Gospel of Sri Ramakrishna gets is that God is not, after all, an unrealisable object living behind the clouds, but our dearest and nearest possession, in whom we live, move, and have our being. There is truly such a thing as God-realisation in this life.

Sri Ramakrishna's first vision of God as we have just seen, was the result of his passionate prayer and fervent desire. He did not follow any particular ritual or ceremony laid down by the scriptures. Thus he showed that the realisation of God is perfectly possible through earnestness alone even if one be not affiliated with any church or religious organisation. Later on, the desire arose in his mind to follow different paths of Hinduism through the rituals prescribed by various teachers for the vision of God. And it may be remarked here that whenever he followed any particular method of discipline, he poured his entire heart into it.

He was a great scientist in the realm of spirituality. He followed to the very letter the disciplines and austerities laid down by his religion. Like all true scientists, he knew that the success of an experiment depends upon the scrupulous observance of its laws. He did not spare himself at all in that direction. Purity became the very breath of his life. Nothing could persuade him to deviate, even by a hair's breadth, from the path of truth in thought, deed and word. To learn humility he would go to the house of a pariah, at dead of night, and clean the dirty places with his long hair. He knew that the two great impediments of spiritual life were lust and gold. He looked upon all women as the manifestation of the Blessed Mother of the Universe and his body would writhe in pain if he touched a coin, even in sleep. As a result of deep discimination he could not see any difference between gold and clay, and found them both equally worthless for the realisation of Truth. Absolutely trustful of the Divine Providence, who hears even the footfall of an ant, he lived from moment to moment depending upon God and without worrying as to what he should eat and drink the next day. His life became a perfect example of resignation and self-surrender to a higher Power who ever cares for our needs. His entire physical and nervous system became attuned to such a high state of consciousness that any contact with objects or thoughts of a worldly nature would give him a strong reaction of pain and suffering. His zeal for the vision of God, which ate him up day by day, beggars all description. While practising spiritual disciplines he forgot food and drink as necessities of life, and sleep he left out altogether. He had only one burning passion, the vision of God. With such a mind he practised different rituals and ceremonies as laid down by Hinduism for spiritual unfoldment. There also he came to the realisation that different paths lead to the same goal.

The friends and relatives of Sri Ramakrishna, unable to realise the meaning of his God-intoxicated state, thought that he had fallen a victim to lunacy. In human society one who does not share the insanity of his neighbours is stigmatised as insane. So they thought that marriage with a suitable girl would help him to get back his normal state of mind. To this suggestion Sri Ramakrishna gave his willing consent, seeing in it also the hand of Providence. When later on, the wife, a pure maiden of sixteen, came to her husband at the Temple of Dakshineswar where Sri Ramakrishna practised his austerities, the saint knelt down before her and said, "The Divine Mother has shown me that every woman is Her manifestation. Therefore I look upon all women as the images of the Divine Mother. I also think of you as such. But I am at your disposal. If you like, you can drag me down to the worldly plane." This girl, during her childhood, used to pray to God, saying,

"O God, make my character as white and fragrant as yonder tuberose. There is a stain even on the moon, but make my life stainless." In the twinkling of an eye, she understood the state of her husband's mind and said with humility that she had no desire to drag him down from the spiritual heights; all that she wanted was the privilege of living near him as his attendant and disciple. When asked about instruction, Sri Ramakrishna said, "God is everybody's beloved, just as the moon is dear to every child. Everyone has an equal right to pray to Him. Out of His grace He manifests Himself to all who call upon Him. You, too, will see Him if you but pray to Him." Henceforth the two souls lived together in the temple-garden as the sharers of many divine visions. Not for a moment would either of them think of any worldly relationship. One night the wife, since adored as the Holy Mother by the numerous devotees of Sri Ramakrishna, asked him while massaging his body, "How do you look upon me?" Sri Ramakrishna replied without a moment's hesitation.

"The Mother who is worshipped in the Temple is the mother who has given birth to this body and is now living in the temple-garden, and she again is massaging my feet at this moment. Verily I always look upon you as the visible representation of the Blissful Mother." Thus Sri Ramakrishna showed by his own life that the mind of a man dwelling in God becomes totally free from all sex-relationship. The same mind which feels a physical urge during the lower state sees the vision of the Divine at the higher level. Lust is not inherent in an object; it is only an idea of the impure mind.

Hitherto Sri Ramakrishna's vision of God was limited to a Personal Deity whom he worshipped alternately as the compassionate Mother or the all-loving Father. In this conception God has human attributes which, according to the religious philosophy of India, is a lower conception of Truth. There is a transcendental aspect of God which defies all human definitions. It is beyond names and forms but is termed Existence, Knowledge and Bliss

Absolute. Realising this, the aspirant transcends the world of multiplicity and merges himself in the Unity of Awareness. Sri Ramakrishna wanted to realise that aspect of the Divine as well. It is a strange phenomenon of his spiritual life that whenever he wanted to pursue a particular spiritual path, a suitable teacher, of his own accord, would come to Dakshineswar. Thus there came to him a monk by the name of Totapuri. This teacher had renounced the world at an early age, did not believe in any worldly relationship, had no earthly possessions, would not stay at one place for more than three days for fear of creating a new attachment and had realised the highest Truth which the philosophers describe as unknown and unknowable for ordinary minds. Through the help of this teacher Sri Ramakrishna realised in three days the Truth which is beyond names and forms and which the Vedas designate as Brahman the Absolute. In this realisation Sri Ramakrishna found the identity of soul and God.

Subsequently he practised the instructions of Christianity and Islam and arrived at the same conclusion. Thus he demonstrated by his own life and inner experience the Truth of his forefathers as laid down in the Vedas: "Reality is One: Sages call It by various names". Sri Ramakrishna also used to say in his own simple and inimitable way: "Different opinions are but different paths, and the goal is one and the same." Rituals and ceremonies, found in all great ancient religions, are external but necessary steps of spiritual growth. They are indispensable for most aspirants during the lower stages of evolution. Like the husks protecting the kernel and falling off when the seed germinates, the rituals and ceremonies also protect the aspirants during the earlier stages and drop off when the Divine Love awakens in their heart.

Having attained the goal of human birth, namely the realisation of Truth, Sri Ramakrishna became eager to share with all this vision of joy and peace. All religious experiences ultimately end in mysticism. But this inspired prophet of the nineteenth century was unlike the mystics who generally go by that name. He did not enter into a cave or lead the life of a recluse, to enjoy, for himself, the bliss of meditation. He realised that he had become an instrument in the hand of God to help his fellow human beings. Thus he wanted one and all to partake of the joy of his realisation. Many a time he prayed thus to the Divine Mother, "Do not make me, O Mother, a cross-grained, pain-hugging recluse. I want to enjoy the world seeing in it Thy manifestation." Drawn by the aroma of his transfigured existence, people began to flock to him from far and near. Men and women, young and old, scientists and agnostics, Christians and Sikhs—people irrespective of their race, creed, caste, or religious affiliation—came to him and felt themselves spiritually uplifted according to their inner evolution. Yet, Sri Ramakrishna was no preacher of the ordinary type. He did not move from the little village of Dakshineswar, did not mount upon a public platform to preach his message and did not advertise himself in the Press. He used to say that the bees come of their own accord in search of honey when the flower is in full bloom.

Among those who came to the saint was a young man who subsequently became world-famous as Swami Vivekananda. Narendranath, as he was then known, represented the spirit of modern times, sceptical, inquisitive, demanding evidence for everything and yet alert and eager to learn Truth. Sri Ramakrishna was the embodiment of the spirit of his ancient religion, self-assured, serene and at peace with himself as the result of his experience of divine Wisdom. He stood at the confluence of these two streams of thought, the ancient and the modern. In answer to the first question of this young man, "Have you seen God?" he gave the emphatic reply that he had seen Him. Though resisting him at every point, ultimately Narendranath became his disciple. Sri Ramakrishna, with the infinite love of a mother and the infinite patience of a teacher, initiated him step by step, into the deepest mysteries of spiritual life. It may be noted here that the teacher did not impose upon the student any blind faith nor demand from him enforced allegience. Sri Ramakrishna, through his superior intellect, satisfied the demands of his disciple's inquisitive mind. Under the direction of his teacher, Swami Vivekananda became the leader of a group of young men who, later on, took the vow of dedicating their lives to the realisation of Truth and service to humanity.

For a quarter of a century this man of God preached his gospel of God-life. Never did he refuse anyone the solace of his instructions, if the seeker was earnest about them. He said, "Where will you find God except in man? Man is the highest manifestation of the Divine. I will give up twenty thousand such bodies to help one man. It is glorious to help even one man." During that period of his spiritual ministration, never a word of condemnation escaped from his blessed lips. He was incapable of seeing evil in others. His whole personality was transfused with love and compassion. Bowing before even the fallen woman, whom society looks down upon as a sinner, he would say, "Thou art also the manifestation of the Divine Mother. In one form thou art standing in the street and in another form thou art worshipped in the temple. I salute Thee." As a result of his constant teaching, he fell a viatrin to cancer of the throat. Even when it became almost impossible for him to swallow liquid food, he could not send away any eager enquirer without some words of solace. One day, during this period, a Yogi remarked that he could easily cure himself through his Yoga powers, by concentrating on the throat. Quick came the reply, "How can my mind, which has been given to God, be directed again to this cage of flesh and blood?" Swami Vivekananda begged him to pray to God for the cure of his ailment. Such a prayer for his own physical body was an impossibility for Sri Ramakrishna. But at the earnest importunity of his disciple, he relaxed. After a while he said to Swami Vivekananda, "Yes, at your request I prayed to the Mother,

'O Mother, on account of pain I cannot eat anything through this mouth. Please relieve my pain if it be Thy pleasure.' She showed you all to me and said, 'Why, are you not eating through all these mouths?" This is a demonstration of how the realisation of God frees the soul from the limitations of the body. At last, on the 16th of August, 1886, Sri Ramakrishna, uttering the sacred name of his beloved God, entered into a state of spiritual ecstasy from which his mind never came back to the mortal plane of existence.

Thus there lived, in our age, a man who saw God face to face. Having realised the fountain of Divine Love, he radiated love for all without any national or geographical limits. Every particle of his being was filled with God-consciousness. Though living in this world, he seemed to be a man of the other world. The man in him was completely transformed into God. Of such, the Vedas declare: "He who realises Truth becomes one with Truth. By the vision of the Divine, man himself becomes Divine."

The life and teachings of this God-man have a tremendous significance for the people of modern times. Living during the transitional period of the nineteenth century when science was most arrogant, and practising austerities in a suburb of Calcutta, the most materialistic city of India, Sri Ramakrishna demonstrated that ideal spiritual life is always possible and that it is not the monopoly of any particular age. The revelation of God takes place at all times and the wind of Divine Mercy never ceases to blow. Who could live, who could breathe if God did not form the very core of our existence? Disciplines laid down by religion can be practised even today if we have the requisite earnestness; and the vision of Truth, revealed to man in olden times, cannot be denied to us now if we are eager for it. On account of its transcendental experience, the life of Sri Ramakrishna is a great challenge to the narrow outlook of our generation. The reader of his life finds undeniable assurance that the highest vision of God is accessible to all as it has been given to him, one of our own times. His life and realisation are not clouded in the haze of mystery and tradition, but have been well sifted in the light of modern reason. The essence of the scentific method consists of experimentation, observation and verification. The science of religion, called Yoga by the Hindus, is based upon this method. Sri Ramakrishna, as a great Yogi, experimented with the spiritual laws without accepting them in blind faith. He observed his own reactions and then came to certain conclusions. The Hindus challenged others also to verify these by their own experimentations and observations. Religion is not occultism or so-called mysticism, but a higher way of life.

God, Sri Ramakrishna has taught us, is not the monopoly of any religion or creed, but the common property of all; He is the loving Father of mankind. He is not only an extracosmic Being, but He permeates the entire universe as intelligence and consciousness. He is present everywhere, from the blade of grass to Brahma as the inmost essence of all. He is the Life and Substratum of all entities, from the atom to the highest Prophet. The same infinite expanse of water forms the basis of the froth, bubbles and mountain-high waves. The difference between man and man, and between other animate and inanimate objects, lies in the degree of divine manifestation. When God is involved, He is the grain of sand, and when He is fully evolved, He is Jesus Christ. Through our strivings and our struggles we are approaching the Central Truth. Art, Science, and Religion are but different expressions of Truth. But one can understand it only when one has realised the Unity of Existence.

Has God any form? Or is He formless? God is both with and without form and yet transcends both. He alone can say what else He is. God with form and God without form are like ice and water. When water freezes into ice it has form. When the same ice is melted into water, all form is lost. God with form and without form are not two different beings. He who is with form is also without form. To a devotee, the worshipper of a

Personal God, He manifests Himself in various forms. Just think of a shoreless ocean—an infinite expanse of water—no land visible in any direction; only here and there are visible blocks of ice formed by intense cold. Similarly under the intensifying influence of the deep devotion of His worshipper, the Infinite reduces Himself, as it were, into the Finite and appears before him as a Being with form. Again, as on the appearance of the sun the ice melts away, so with the awakening of knowledge, God with form melts away into the Formless. The water of the ocean, when viewed from a distance, appears to have a dark-blue colour, but becomes colourless when taken in the hand; in the same way God is also associated with a definite colour and complexion from a distance, but He is the attributeless Truth when the devotee merges in Him.

Religion does not consist of dogmas and creeds. It is Realisation. It is being and becoming. No one can ever put any finality upon God's nature. It is beyond the conception of our relative mind. We grasp only a limited aspect of God according to our mental development. Sri Ramakrishna used to say that everything in the world—the words of saints, the statements of the scriptures—has been polluted like food thrown from the mouth; but God alone is unpolluted as no human tongue has been able to describe fully what He is. His nature can be known only in the silent depth of our heart. Again, Sri Ramakrishna said that once a doll, made of salt, wanted to measure the depth of the ocean; but no sooner did it touch the water than it melted in the ocean. How could it tell about the depth? Similarly, neither the mind nor words can express the real nature of God when the aspirant has merged in Him. A text of the Vedas says: "The words come back with the mind vainly trying to express what Truth is."

What is the relation of God to man? This is the moot question of religion. Sri Ramakrishna said in a simple way that when we consider ourselves as physical beings, then God is the Master and the Father and we are

His servants or children. When we look upon ourselves as embodied souls, then God is the Universal Soul and we are Its emanations. Like fire and its sparks, God and man possess the same attributes and qualities. But when we think of ourselves as Spirit, then we are identical with God—the one and the same Spirit, birthless, deathless, causeless, and infinite. Prof. Max Muller wrote that Sri Ramakrishna's simple words and illustrations have such a force of directness and irresistibility because his mind was unspoiled by any academic education. They were the outcome of his direct experience.

The four cardinal points of Sri Ramakrishna's teachings are the Oneness of Existence, Divinity of Man, Unity of God, and the Harmony of Religions. The entire universe is one—not only as a stretch of matter or idea but also as Indivisible Spirit. The multiplicity of names and forms, created by our ignorance, vanishes at the dawn of Divine Knowledge. The cherished treasures of human progress, such as love, understanding, unselfishness and other ethical principles, can be explained only from the standpoint of this Unity. Otherwise there is no room for fellow-feeling in a world of multiplicity, governed by lifeless natural laws. This Unity comprehends all objects, animate and inanimate, as well as men and angels.

Man is divine by nature. Either as created in the image of God, or as His spark or as one with Him, the essential nature of man can never lose this perfection. There is no such thing as sin which can change the quality of the soul. The wicked action of a man may impose a veil upon his divine nature but can never destroy it. God exists in us as potentia and possibility. An action is called good or moral that helps us to re-discover this hidden Divinity. And an action is immoral or bad which conjures up before us the appearance of manifoldness. The experiences we gather at the physical, mental or aesthetic level do not belong to our real soul. They may be called, at best, a mixure of Truth and falsehood. Through this inscrutable ignorance we behave as if we were corporeal beings. We have hypnotised ourselves into thinking that we are imperfect and limited and that we exist in time and space, subject to the law of causation. The aim of religion is to dehypnotise ourselves and make us aware of our divine heritage.

God is one and indivisible. The different gods of religion and mythology are but different aspects of the Absolute as comprehended by finite human minds. Father in Heaven, just and moral Governor, Eternal Spirit, Nirvāna or the extinction of desires, Light, Law, *etc.*, are but different facets of the one Godhead. He is all these and infinitely more than the human mind can think. The God that is defined as the goal of different religions is only the highest reading of the Absolute by the finite human mind and expressed through imperfect human language.

The greatest contribution of Sri Ramakrishna to the modern world, torn by theological quarrels, is the Harmony of Religions. Each great ancient religion has three steps, namely, ritual, mythology and philosophy. The first two are the externals of religion, and philosophy is its basis. There can never by any uniformity in rituals and mythologies. These are the abstract ideas of philosophy made concrete for the grasp of ordinary minds. They are to be given up when the soul, through its purity and discipline, is able to comprehend the essence of religion. Religious quarrels arise when we insist that the externals of religion are to be kept forever. As Swami Vivekananda used to say, a man must be born in a church but he must not die in a church. There never has been my religion or your religion, my national religion or your national religion, but there is only one Eternal Religion of which different religions are but different manifestations to suit different temperaments. It is not the case that this religion or that religion is true in this or that respect, but the fact is that all religions are efficacious in all respects as suited to diverse conditions of our mind. If one religion is true then all religions are equally so. But if one religion proves false then all religions fall to the ground. Men quarrel about religions because they emphasise personalities, words and explanations and never go to the fountainhead. We are quarrelling about the empty baskets while the contents have slipped into the ditch. Different religions are but different forces in the economy of God. They are necessary to maintain the equilibrium of the world and enhance the richness of creation. They are not antagonistic but complementary. Like the different photographs of a building taken from different angles, different religions also give us the picture of one Truth from different standpoints. Various religions are but flowers of different colours which we should tie with the cord of love into a beautiful bouquet and offer at the altar of Truth. By the test of the survival of the fittest the great ancient religions of the world do justify their existence and usefulness. Therefore Sri Ramakrishna's attitude towards other religions is not that of toleration which implies viewing faiths other than one's own as if they were inferior. His ideal is that of acceptance. To him all religions are the revelation of God in His diverse aspects to satisfy the manifold demands of human minds. One day a young disciple criticised before him the questionable methods of a religious sect. Sri Ramakrishna said, "That is also a pathway to reach God. To enter a house there are many doors. There are front doors, side-doors and there is also a backdoor. But you need not go in by that door." As a result of his spiritual experiences he came to the conclusion that there are not only many mansions in the Father's House, but there are also many doors leading thereto.

What is the utility of religious experiences in our daily and practical life? If man were only an animal with eating, drinking and sleeping propensities, satisfied with a little display of reason and the solution of some intellectual problems, then perhaps, there would be no meaning in his excursion into the realm of Spirit. But the infinite nature of the human soul can never be happy with the finite experiences of life. Through the travail of our finite experience and knowledge we are trying to reach the Infinite. The whole life of man is the play of the Infinite in the finite. Therefore any experience of life devoid of the touch of the Divine is barren and futile. The drab and grey of life can be illumined by the sunrise glow of divine experience. It invests life with a new meaning and dignity. What does it avail a man if he gains the whole world but loses his soul? Nothing else matters if the touch of God is felt in our daily activities. And what else does matter if we do not feel that indwelling Presence in our everyday action? Mind without the touch of the Divine roams aimlessly in the blind alleys of the world. Therefore Sri Ramakrishna used to say, "Do whatever you please, with the knowledge of God in your pocket."

Mind uninspired by Divine Wisdom is like milk that gets easily mixed up with the water of the world. But if by churning, one transforms milk into butter, then it floats on the water. In the same way we are to purify the mind by divine knowledge; and then if it dwells in the world it will not be polluted by worldliness. And again, as our saints used to say, as long as we spin around holding fast to a post, there is no danger of our falling to the ground. In the same way, if we work in the world with our mind steadfastly devoted to God, there is no risk of losing ourselves in confusion. "Be like a wet nurse," Sri Ramakrishna said, "who takes care of her master's children as her own, but in her heart of hearts knows that she has no claim upon them; so think also that you are but the trustees and guardians of your people, but the real Master is God Himself." We are all instruments in the hands of God who has assigned to us our respective duties for the discipline of our heart. Religious life does not mean the shirking of duties or avoidance of responsibilities. The same Truth manifests Itself as our inner vision and the external manifold. As such there is no intrinsic difference between the sacerdotal and the secular. Everything is sacred. There is no difference between the temple and the farm-yard. The cloister and the laboratory, the temple and the studio, the cell and the market-place are equally fit places of worship. To accept life after transcending its limitations is the last divine sacrifice. To labour is to pray. To have and hold is as stern a trust as to quit and avoid. Life itself is Religion. True to this ideal of its partron Saint, the Ramakrishna Mission has the twin methods of discipline, namely 'work' and 'worship'; or rather its members say that 'work is worship'. One day when young Swami Vivekananda begged his Master to grant him the boon of a spiritual ecstasy in which the disciple could keep his mind above for four or five days together, coming down occasionally to the physical plane for a few minutes to eat some morsels of food, Sri Ramakrishna answered reproachfully, 'Why are you so anxious to see God with your eyes closed? Can't you see Him with your eyes open? Worship God through suffering humanity."

Great Prophets like Sri Ramakrishna are born now and then to demonstrate the eternal truths of Religion. There may be nothing new in what he preached and taught. Without him Hindu religion would have been equally valid today as it has been for the past thousands of years. The spiritual texts, without him, would have carried equal weight with students who care for them. But in Sri Ramakrishna we have the revealer and modern interpreter of the spiritual truths about which our minds may be in doubt for want of actual demonstration. Like the giant American hickory tree, he stands raising his head above the storms of doubt and scepticism. He has laid emphasis on those aspects of religion which we can grasp and follow in our modern daily life. Above all, he is a figure in history and his life is not obscured by doubtful myths. He stands as the justification of not only the Hindu faith but of the life of the Spirit in general. His realisations furnish us with the master-key by which we can unlock every door in the mansion of Spirit. His teachings act like a powerful searchlight by which we can see through the mummeries and externals of religion and discern its innermost essence. This Prophet of the nineteenth century did not found any cult nor did he show a new path to salvation. When under the relentless sledge-hammer blows of modern thought our cherished ideals of the time-honoured ancient faiths began to crumble, Sri Ramakrishna, by his own life, has demonstrated the validity and truth of the Prophets and Saviours of the past and thus restored the falling edifice of Religion upon a new and more secure foundation.[1]

1. An address delivered by Swami Nikhilananda at New York on the occasion of Sri Ramakrishna Centenary in 1936.

तव कथामृतं तप्तजीवनं कविभिरीडितं कल्मषापहम् ।
श्रवणमङ्गलं श्रीमदाततं भुवि गृणन्ति ते भूरिदा जनाः ॥

The nectar of your story,
the praise of poet-seers,
Elixir to parched souls,
delight of listening ears,
The cleanser out of sin,
is grand and glorious;
They who spread it
wide on earth
are generous.

Srimad Bhagavatam 10.31. 9

Book First

The World

THIS IS INDEED THE WORLD!

Once Hriday[1] brought a bull-calf here. I saw, one day, that he had tied it with a rope in the garden[2], so that it might graze there. I asked him, "Hriday, why do you tie the calf there every day?" "Uncle" he said, "I am going to send the calf to our village. When it grows strong I shall yoke it to the plough." As soon as I heard these words I was stunned to think: "How inscrutable is the play of the Divine Maya! Kamarpukur[3] and Sihore[4] are so far away from Calcutta! This poor calf must go all that way. Then it will grow, and at length it will be yoked to the plough. This is indeed the world! This is indeed maya!" I fell

---

1. A nephew of Sri Ramakrishna. Hriday attended on the Master for a long time.

2. Temple garden of Dakshineswar, where Sri Ramakrishna lived.

3. A village in Bengal, where Sri Ramakrishna was born.

4. Native village of Hriday.

unconscious. Only after a long time did I regain consciousness. (1)

IN THE FOREST OF THE WORLD

ONCE a man was going through a forest, when three robbers fell upon him and robbed him of all his possessions. One of the robbers said, "What's the use of keeping this man alive?" So saying, he was about to kill him with his sword, when the second robber interrupted him, saying: "Oh! no! What is the use of killing him? Tie him hand and foot and leave him here." The robbers bound his hands and feet and went away. After a while the third robber returned and said to the man: "Ah, I am sorry. Are you hurt? I will release you from your bonds." After setting the man free, the thief said: "Come with me. I will take you to the public highway." After a long time they reached the road. At this the man said: "Sir, you have been very good to me. Come with me to my house." "Oh, no!" the robber replied. "I can't go there. The police will know it."

This world itself is the forest. The three robbers prowling here are sattva, rajas, and tamas. It is they that rob a man of the Knowledge of Truth. Tamas wants to destroy him. Rajas binds him to the world. But sattva rescues him from the clutches of rajas and tamas. Under the protection of sattva, man is rescued from anger, passion and other evil effects of tamas. Further, sattva also is a robber. It cannot give man the ultimate Knowledge of Truth, though it shows him the road leading to the Supreme Abode of God. Setting him on the path, sattva tells him: "Look yonder. There is your home." Even sattva is far away from the knowledge of Brahman. (2)

WHAT THE WORLD MAKES OF MEN

As a boy, at Kamarpukur, I loved Ram Mallick dearly. But afterwards, when he came here, I couldn't touch him. Ram Mallick and I were great friends during our boyhood. We were together day and night; we slept together. At that time I was sixteen or seventeen years old. People used to say, "If one of them were a woman they would marry each other."

Both of us used to play at his house. I remember those days very well. His relatives used to come riding in palanquins. Now he has a shop at Chanak. I sent for him many a time; he came here the other day and spent two days. Ram said he had no children; he brought up his nephew, but the boy died. He told me this with a sigh; his eyes were filled with tears; he was grief stricken for his nephew. He said further that since they had no children of their own, all his wife's affection had been turned to the nephew. She was completely overwhelmed with grief. Ram said to her: "You are crazy. What will you gain by grieving? Do you want to go to Benares?" You see, he called his wife crazy. Grief for the boy totally 'diluted' him. I found he had no stuff within him. I couldn't touch him. (3)

Men of the World

WHEN THEY ARE ANNOYED

You see, we don't take any collection during the performance at our place. Jadu's[1] mother says to me, "Other sadhus always ask for money, but you do not." Worldly people feel annoyed if they have to spend money.

A theatrical performance was being given at a certain place. A man felt a great desire to take a seat and see it. He peeped in and saw that a collection was being taken from the audience. Quietly he slipped away. Another performance was being given at some other place. He went there and, inquiring, found that no collection would be taken. There was a great rush of people. He elbowed his way through the crowd and reached the centre of the hall. There he picked out a nice seat for

1. A devotee of Sri Ramakrishna.

himself, twirled his moustaches, and sat through the performance. (4)

WHEN ALL TEETH FEEL

LET me tell you a story. A man used to celebrate the Durga Puja at his house with great pomp. Goats were sacrificed from sunrise to sunset. But after a few years the sacrifice was not so imposing. Then some one said to him, "How is it, sir, that the sacrifice at your place has become such a tame affair?" "Don't you see?" he said, "My teeth are gone now." (5)

THERE ARE SUCH MEN INDEED!

IT is not mentioned in their 'Science' that God can take human form; so how can they believe it? There are such men indeed!

Listen to a story. A man said to his friend, "I have just seen a house fall down with a terrific crash." Now, the friend to whom he told this had received an English education. He said: "Just a minute. Let me look it up in the newspaper." He read the paper but could not find the news of a house falling down with a crash. Thereupon he said to his friend; "Well,

I don't believe you. It isn't in the paper; so it is all false." (6)

THE JACKAL THAT WON'T LEAVE
THE COMPANY OF A BULLOCK

ONCE a jackal saw a bullock and would not give up his company. The bullock roamed about and the jackal followed him. The jackal thought: "There hang the bullock's testicles. Sometime or other they will drop to the ground and I shall eat them." When the bullock slept on the ground, the jackal lay down too, and when the bullock moved about, the jackal followed him. Many days passed in this way, but the bullock's testicles still clung to his body. The jackal went away disappointed.

That also happens to flatterers. They think that the rich man will loosen his purse-strings for them. But it is very difficult to get anything from him. (7)

THE PLUNDERERS WHO GO
ABOUT AS RELIGIOUS

THERE was a goldsmith who kept a jewelry shop. He looked like a great devotee, a true

Vaishnava, with beads round his neck, rosary in his hand, and the holy marks on his forehead. Naturally people trusted him and came to his shop on business. They thought that, being such a pious man, he would never cheat them. Whenever a party of customers entered the shop, they would hear one of his craftsmen say, 'Kesava! Kesava!' Another would say after a while, 'Gopal! Gopal!' Then a third would mutter, 'Hari! Hari!' Finally someone would say, 'Hara! Hara!' Now these are, as you know, different names of God. Hearing so much chanting of God's names the customers naturally thought that this goldsmith must be a very superior person. But can you guess the goldsmith's true intention? The man who said 'Kesava! Kesava!' meant to ask, '*Who are these?*—Who are these customers?' The man who said 'Gopal! Gopal!' conveyed the idea that the customers were merely *a herd of cows.* That was the estimate he formed of them after the exchange of a few words. The man who said 'Hari! Hari!' asked, 'Since they are no better than a herd of cows, then *may we rob them?'* He who said 'Hara! Hara!' gave his assent, meaning by these words, *'Do rob* by all means, since they are mere cows!' (8)

HOW THEY QUARREL!

IT is not good to say that what we ourselves think of God is the only truth and what others think is false; that because we think of God as formless, therefore He is formless and cannot have any form; that because we think of God as having form, therefore He has form and cannot be formless. Can a man really fathom God's nature?

This kind of friction exists between the Vishnava and the Sāktas. The Vaishnava says, 'My Kesava is the only Saviour', whereas the Sākta insists, 'My Bhagavati is the only Saviour.'

Once I took Vaishnavacharan[1] to Mathur[2] Babu. Mathur welcomed him with great

1. A contemporary of Sri Ramakrishna

2. The son-in-law of Rani Rasmani, the foundress of the Kali Temple at Dakshineswar, where Sri Ramakrishna lived and did his Sadhana.

courtesy and fed him from silver plates. Now, Vaishnavacharan was a very learned Vaishnava and an orthodox devotee of his sect. Mathur, on the other hand, was a devotee of the Divine Mother. They were engaged in a friendly discussion when suddenly Vaishnavacharan said, "Kesava is the only Saviour." No sooner did Mathur hear this than his face became red with anger and he blurted out, "You rascal!" He was a Sākta. Wasn't it natural for him to say like that? I gave Vaishnavacharan a nudge! (9)

A WORLDLING IS A POOR EXPONENT OF THE SASTRAS

A MAN wanted to engage a *Bhāgavata* pandit who could explain the *Bhāgavata* to him. His friend said: "I know of an excellent pandit. But there is one difficulty: he does a great deal of farming. He has four ploughs and eight bullocks and is always busy with them; he has no leisure." Thereupon the man said: "I don't care for a pandit who has no leisure. I am not looking for a *Bhāgavata* scholar burdened with ploughs and bullocks. I want a pandit who can really expound the sacred book to me." (10)

ELDER, THE PUMPKIN CUTTER

YOU must have seen the sort of elderly man who lives in a family and is always ready, day and night, to entertain the children. He sits in the parlour and smokes the hubble-bubble. With nothing in particular to do, he leads a lazy life. Now and again he goes to the inner court and cuts a pumpkin; for since women do not cut pumpkins, they send the children to ask him to come and do it. This is the extent of his usefulness—hence his nick-name, 'Elder, the pumpkin cutter."

He is neither a man of the world nor a devotee of God. That is not good. (11)

THERE IS NEED FOR EVERYTHING

WICKED People are needed too.

At one time the tenants of an estate became unruly. The landlord had to send Golak Choudhury, who was a ruffian. He was such a hard administrator that the tenants trembled at the very mention of the name.

There is need for everything. Once Sita said to her husband: "Rama, it would be grand if every house in Ayodhya were a mansion! I find many houses are old and dilapidated." "But, my dear," said Rama, "if all the houses were beautiful ones, what would the masons do?" God has created all kinds of things. He has created good trees and poisonous plants and weeds as well. Among the animals there are good, bad, and all kinds of creatures—tigers, lions, snakes, and so on. (12)

THERE ARE MEN AND MEN

MEN may be divided into four classes: those bound by the fetters of the world, the seekers after liberation, the liberated, and the everfree. Among the everfree we may count sages like Narada. They live in the world for the good of others, to teach men spiritual truths. Those in bondage are sunk in worldliness and are forgetful of God.

The seekers after liberation want to free themselves from attachment to the world. Some of them succeed and others do not.

The liberated souls, such as the Sadhus and Mahatmas, are not entangled in the world, in 'woman and gold.' Their minds are free from worldliness. Besides they always meditate on the Lotus Feet of God.

Suppose a net has been cast into a lake to catch fish. Some fish are so clever that they are never caught in the net. They are like the everfree. But most of the fish are entangled in the net. Some of them try to free themselves from it, and they are like those who seek liberation. But not all the fish that struggle succeed. A very few do jump out of the net, making a big splash in the water. Then the fishermen shout, 'Look! There goes a big one!' But most of the fish caught in the net cannot escape, nor do they make any effort to get out. On the contary, they burrow into the mud with the net in their mouths and lie there quietly, thinking, 'We need not fear any more; we are quite safe here.' But the poor things do not know that the fishermen will drag them out with the net. These are like the men bound to the world. (13)

The Bane of Worldliness

THE ROOT OF ALL TROUBLES

In a certain place the fishermen were catching fish. A kite swooped down and snatched a fish. At the sight of the fish, about a thousand crows chased the kite and made a great noise with their cawing. Whichever way the kite flew with the fish, the crows followed it. The kite flew to the south and the crows followed it there. The kite flew to the the north and still the crows followed after it. The kite went east and west, but with the same result. As the kite began to fly about in confusion, lo, the fish dropped from its mouth. The crows at once let the kite alone and flew after the fish. Thus relieved of its worries, the kite sat on the branch of a tree and thought: 'That wretched fish was the root of all my troubles. I have now got rid of it and therefore I am at peace.'

As long as a man has the fish, that is, worldly desires, he must perform actions and consequently suffer from worry, anxiety, and restlessness. No sooner does he renounce these desires than his activities fall away and he enjoys peace of soul. (14)

ALL FOR A SINGLE PIECE OF LOIN-CLOTH

A SADHU under the instruction of his Guru built for himself a small shed, thatched with leaves at a distance from the haunts of men. He began his devotional exercises in this hut. Now, every morning after ablution he would hang his wet cloth and the kaupina (loin-cloth) on a tree close to the hut, to dry them. One day on his return from the neighbouring village, which he would visit to beg for his daily food, he found that the rats had cut holes in his kaupina. So the next day he was obliged to go to the village for a fresh one. A few days later, the sadhu spread his loin-cloth on the roof of his hut to dry it and then went to the village to beg as usual. On his return he found that the rats had torn it into shreds. He felt much annoyed and thought within himself, "Where shall I go again to beg for a rag? Whom shall I ask for one?" All the same he saw the villagers the next day and represented to them the mischief done by the rats. Having heard all he had to say, the villagers said, "Who will keep you supplied with cloth every day? Just do one thing—keep a cat; it will keep away the rats." The sadhu forthwith secured a kitten in the village and carried it to his hut. From that day the rats ceased to trouble him and there was no end to his joy. The sadhu now began to tend the useful little creature with great care and feed it on the milk begged from the village. After some days, a villager said to him: "Sadhuji, you require milk every day; you can supply your want for a few days at most by begging; who will supply you with milk all the year round? Just do one thing—keep a cow. You can satisfy your own creature comforts by drinking its milk and you can also give some to your cat." In a few days the sadhu procured a milch cow and had no occasion to beg for milk any more. By and by, the sadhu found it necessary to beg for straw for his cow. He had to visit the neighbouring villages for the purpose, but the villagers said, "There are lots of uncultivated lands close to your hut; just cultivate the land and you shall not have to beg for straw for your cow." Guided by their advice, the sadhu took to tilling the land. Gradually he had to engage some labourers and later on found it necessary to build barns to store the crop in. Thus he became, in course of time, a sort of landlord. And, at last he had to take a wife to look after his big household. He now passed his days just like a busy householder.

After some time, his Guru came to see him. Finding himself surrounded by goods and chattels, the Guru felt puzzled and enquired of a servant, "An ascetic used to live here in a hut; can you tell me where he has removed himself?" The servant did not know what to say in reply. So the Guru ventured to enter into the house, where he met his disciple. The Guru said to him. "My son, what is all this?" The disciple, in great shame, fell at the feet of his Guru and said, "My Lord, all for a single piece of loin-cloth!" (15)

THE TIGER THAT LURKS BEHIND WORLDLY JOYS

GOD is like the wish-yielding tree of the celestial world (Kalpataru), which gives whatever one asks of it. So one should be careful to give up all worldly desires when one's mind has been purified by religious exercises.

Just listen to a story: A certain traveller came to a large plain in the course of his travels. As he had been walking in the sun for many hours, he was thoroughly exhausted and heavily perspiring; so he sat down in the shade of a tree to rest a little. Presently he began to think what a comfort it would be if he could but get a soft bed there to sleep on. He was not aware that he was sitting under the celestial tree. As soon as the above thought rose in his mind, he found a nice bed by his side. He felt much astonished, but all the same stretched himself on it. Now he thought to himself how pleasant it would be were a young damsel to come there and gently stroke his legs. No sooner did the thought arise in his mind than he found a young damsel sitting at his feet and stroking his legs. The traveller felt supremely happy. Presently he felt hungry and thought: "I have got whatever I have wished for; could I not then get some food?" Instantly he found various kinds of delicious food spread before him. He at once fell to eating, and having helped himself to his heart's content, stretched himself again on his bed. He now began to revolve in his mind the events of the day. While thus occupied, he thought, "If a tiger should attack me all of a sudden!" In an instant a large tiger jumped on him and broke his neck and began to drink his blood. In this way the traveller lost his life.

Such is the fate of men in general. If during your meditation you pray for men or money or worldly honours, your desires will no doubt be satisfied to some extent; but, mind you, there is the dread of the tiger behind the gifts you get. Those tigers—disease, bereavements, loss of honour and wealth etc.,—are a thousand times more terrible than the live tiger. (16)

THAT OPPRESSING STENCH OF WORLDLINESS

ONCE a fish wife was a guest in the house of a gardener who raised flowers. She came there with her empty basket, after selling fish in the market, and was asked to sleep in a room where flowers were kept. But, because of the fragrance of the flowers, she couldn't get to sleep for a long time! She was restless and began to fidget about. Her hostess saw her condition and said, "Hello! Why are you tossing from side to side so restlessly?" The fishwife said: "I don't know, friend. Perhaps the smell of the flowers has been disturbing my sleep. Can you give me my fish-basket? Perhaps that will put me to sleep." The basket was brought to her. She sprinkled water on it and set it near her nose. Then she fell sound asleep and snored all night. (17)

WORLDLY GOODS ARE NOT THINE FOR EVER

THE steward of a certain rich man was left in charge of his master's property. When asked by someone as to whose property it was, he used to say: "Sir, this is all my property; these houses and these gardens are all mine." He would speak in this strain and go about with an air of vanity. One day he happened to catch fish in a pond of his master's garden-house in contravention of his strict prohibition. As ill-luck would have it, the master came upon the scene just then, and saw what his dishonest steward was doing. Finding out the faithlessness of his servant, the master at once drove him away from his estate, disgraced and dishonoured, and confiscated all his past earning. The poor fellow could not take with him even his rickety box of utensils which was his sole private property.

Such is the punishment that overtakes false pride. (18)

THE JAR OF DESIRE CAN NEVER BE FILLED UP

A BARBER who was passing under a haunted tree, heard a voice say, "Will you accept seven jars full of gold?" The barber looked around, but could see no one. The offer of seven jars of gold, however, roused his cupidity, and he cried aloud, "Yes, I shall accept the seven jars." At once came the reply, "Go home, I have carried the jars to your house." The barber ran home in hot haste to verify the truth of this strange announcement. And when he entered the house, he saw the jars before him. He opened them and found them all full of gold, except the last one which was only half-full. A strong desire now arose in the barber's mind to fill the seventh jar also; for without it his happiness was incomplete. He therefore converted all his ornaments into gold coins and put them into the jar; but the mysterious vessel was, as before, unfilled. This exasperated the barber. Starving himself and his family, he saved some amount more and tried to fill the jar; but the jar remained as before. So one day he humbly requested the king to increase his pay, as his income was not sufficient to maintain himself. Now the barber was a favourite of the king, and as soon as the request was made the king doubled his pay. All this pay he saved and put into the jar, but the greedy jar showed no signs of filling. At last he began to live by begging from door to door, and his professional income and the income from begging—all went into the insatiable cavity of the mysterious jar. Months passed, and the condition of the miserable and miserly barber grew worse every day. Seeing his sad plight the king asked him one day: "Hallo! When your pay was half of what you now get, you were happy, cheerful and contented; but with double that pay, I see you morose, care-worn and dejected. What is the matter with you? Have you got 'the seven jars'?" The barber was taken aback by this question and replied, "Your Majesty, who has informed you of this?" The king said: "Don't you know that these are the signs of the person to whom the Yaksha consigns the seven jars. He offered me also the same jars, but I asked him whether this money might be spent or was merely to be hoarded. No sooner had I asked this question than the Yaksha ran away without any reply. Don't you know that no one can spend that money? It only brings with it the desire of hoarding. Go at once and return the money." The barber was brought to his senses by this advice, and he went to the haunted tree and said, "Take back your gold, O Yaksha." The Yaksha replied, "All right." When the barber returned home, he found that the seven jars had vanished as mysteriously as they were brought in, and with it also had vanished his life-long savings.

Those who do not understand the difference between what is real expenditure and what is real income, lose all they have. (19)

WHY YOGI SLIPS DOWN FROM HIS YOGA

AT Kamarpukur I have seen the mongoose living in its hole up in the wall. It feels snug there. Sometimes people tie a brick to its tail; then the pull of the brick makes it come out of its hole. Everytime the mongoose tries to be comfortable inside the hole, it has to come out because of the pull of the brick.

Such is the effect of brooding on worldly objects that it makes the yogi stray from the path of yoga. (20)

THOSE WORTHLESS THINGS!

BODY and wealth are impermanent. Why go to take so much trouble for their sakes? Just think of the plight of the Hatha yogis. Their attention is fixed on one ideal only—longevity. They do not aim at the realization of God at all. They practise such exercise as washing out the intestines, drinking milk through a tube, and the like, with that one aim in view.

There was once a goldsmith whose tongue suddenly turned up and stuck to his palate. He looked like a man in Samadhi. He became completely inert and remained so a long time. People came to worship him. After several years, his tongue suddenly returned to its natural position, and he became conscious of things as before. So he went back to his work as before.

These are physical things and have nothing to do with God. There was a man who knew eighty-two postures and talked big about yoga-samadhi. But inwardly he was drawn to 'woman and gold'. Once he found a bank-note worth several thousand rupees. He could not resist the temptation, and swallowed it, thinking he would get it out somehow later on. The note was got out of him alright, but he was sent to jail for three years. (21)

Kama-Kanchana[1]

(LUST AND GOLD)

COURT MARRIAGE AND YOU COURT SERVITUDE

It is 'woman and gold' that binds man and robs him of his freedom. It is woman that creates the need for gold. For woman one becomes the slave of another, and so loses his freedom. Then he cannot act as he likes.

The priests in the temple of Govindaji at Jaipur were celibates at first, and at that time they had fiery natures. Once the King of Jaipur sent for them, but they didn't obey him. They said to the messenger, "Ask the king to come to see us." After consultation, the king and his ministers arranged marriages for them. From then on the king didn't have to send for them. They would come to him of themselves and say: "Your Majesty, we have come with our blessings. Here are the sacred flowers of the temple. Deign to accept them." They came to the palace, for now they always wanted money for this thing or another—the building of a house, the rice-taking ceremony of their babies, or the rituals connected with the beginning of their children's education. (22)

THE FALL OF THE TWELVE HUNDRED

THERE is the story of twelve hundred nedas[1] and thirteen hundred nedis[2]. Virabhadra, the son of Nityananda Goswami had thirteen hundred 'shaven headed' disciples. They attained great spiritual powers. That alarmed their teacher. "My disciples have acquired great spiritual powers," thought Virabhadra. "Whatever they say to people will come to pass. Wherever they go they may create alarming situations; for people offending them unwittingly will come to grief." Thinking thus, Virabhadra one day called them to him and said, "See me after performing your daily devotions on the banks of the Ganges." These disciples had such high spiritual nature that,

1. Literally, "Shaven headed", indicative of absolute renunciation of 'lust and gold'.

2. Vaishnava nuns.

while meditating, they would go into samadhi and be unaware of the river-water flowing over their heads during the flood-tide. Then the ebb-tide would come and still they would remain absorbed in meditation.

Now, one hundred of these disciples had anticipated what their teacher would ask of them. Lest they should have to disobey his injunctions, they had quickly disappeared from the place before he summoned them. So they did not go to Virabhadra with others. The remaining twelve hundred disciples went to the teacher after finishing their morning meditations. Virabhadra said to them: "These thirteen hundred nuns will serve you. I ask you to marry them." "As you please, revered sir," they said, "But one hundred of us have gone way." Thenceforth each of these twelve hundred disciples had a wife. Consequently they all lost their spiritual power. Their austerities did not have their original fire. The company of women robbed them of their spirituality because it destroyed their freedom. (23)

MASTER OF EVERYTHING, SLAVE OF SEX!

A JOB-SEEKER got tired of visiting the manger in an office. He couldn't get the job. The manager said to him, "There is no vacancy now; but come and see me now and then." This went on for a long time, and the candidate lost all hope.

One day he told his tale of woe to a friend. The friend said: "How stupid you are! Why are you wearing away the soles of your feet going to that fellow? You had better go to Golap. You will get the job tomorrow." "Is that so?" said the candidate. "I am going right away." Golap was the manager's mistress. The candidate called on her and said: "Mother, I am in great distress. You must help me out of it. I am the son of a poor brahmana. Where else shall I go for help? Mother, I have been out of work many days. My children are about to strave to death. I can get a job if you but say a word."

Golap said to him, "Child, whom should I speak to?" She said to herself: "Ah, the poor brahmana! He has been suffering too much."

The candidate said to her, "I am sure to get the job if you just put in a word about it to the manager." Golap said, "I shall speak to him today and settle the matter." The very next morning a man called on the candidate and said, "You are to work in the manager's office, from today." The manager said to his English boss: "This man is very competent. I have appointed him. He will do credit to the firm."

24

BHAGAVATA IN THE EAR, BROTHEL IN THE MIND

ONCE two friends were going along the street when they saw some people listening to a reading of the *Bhagavata*. "Come, friend," said the one to the other, "let us hear the sacred book." So saying he went in and sat down. The second man peeped in and went away. He entered a house of ill-fame. But very soon he felt disgusted with the place. "Shame on me!" he said to himself. "My friend has been listening to the sacred word of Hari; and see where I am!" But the friend who had been listening to the Bhagavata also became disgusted.

"What a fool I am!" he said. "I have been listening to this fellow's blah-blah, and my friend is having a grand time." In course of time they both died. The messenger of death came for the soul of one who had listened to the *Bhagavata* and dragged it off to hell. The messenger of God came for the soul of the one who had been to the house of prostitution and led it up to heaven.

Verily, the Lord looks into a man's heart and does not judge him by what he does or where he lives. (25)

GREATER EVEN THAN THE GURU!

A POOR brahmana had a rich cloth merchant as his disciple. The merchant was very miserly by nature. One day the brahmana was in need of a small piece of cloth for covering his sacred book. He went to his disciple and asked for the required piece of cloth; but the merchant replied: "I am very sorry, sir. Had you told me of this a few hours earlier, I would have given you the thing wanted. Unfortunately, now I have no small piece of cloth which will answer your purpose. However, I shall remember your requirement, but please remind me of it now and then." The brahmana had to go away disappointed. This conversation between the guru and his worthy disciple was overheard by the wife of the latter from behind a screen. She at once sent a man after the brahmana, and calling him inside the house, said, "Revered Father, what is it that you were asking from the master of the house?" The brahmana related all that had happened. The wife said: "Please go home sir; you will get the cloth tomorrow morning." When that merchant returned home at night the wife asked him, "Have you closed your shop?" The merchant said, "Yes, what is the matter?" She said, "Go at once and bring two cloths of the best quality in the shop." He said, "Why this hurry? I shall give you the best cloth tomorrow morning." The wife, however, insisted, "No, I must have them just now or not at all." What could the poor merchant do? The person whom he had now to deal with was not the spiritual guru whom he could send away with vague and indefinite promises, but the 'curtain guru' whose behests must be instantaneously obe-yed, or else there would be no peace for him at home. At last the merchant, willingly enough, opened the shop, at that late hour of the night, and brought the cloths for her. Early next morning, the good lady sent the article to the guru with the message, "If in future you want anything from us, ask me, and you will get it." (26)

MODERN JANAKAS!

A GENTLEMAN of modern education was once discussing with the Master the nature of house-holders uncontaminated by worldliness. To him, the Master said, "I know of what sort is your 'uncontaminated family-man' of the present day! If a poor brahmana comes to beg of this master of the house, he (being an uncontaminated family-man and having no concern with money matters, for it is his wife who manages all those things!) says to the begging brahmana, 'Sir, I never touch money, why do you waste your time in begging of me?' The brahmana, however, proves inexorable. Fired with his importunate entreaties your uncontaminated family-man thinks within himself that he must be paid a rupee, and tells him openly: 'Well, sir, come tomorrow, I shall see what I can do for you.' Then going in, this typical house-holder tells his wife, 'Look here, my dear, a poor brahmana is in great distress; let us give him a rupee.'

Hearing the word 'rupee' his wife gets out of temper and says tauntingly, 'Aha, what a generous fellow you are! Are rupees like leaves and straws to be thrown away without the least thought?' 'Well, my dear,' replies the master in an apologetic tone, 'the brahmana is very poor and we should not give him less.' 'No,' says his wife, 'I cannot spare so much. Here is a two anna bit; you can give that to him, if you like.' As the Babu is a family-man quite uncontaminated by worldliness, he takes, of course, what his wife gives him, and next day the beggar gets only a two anna piece.

So you see, your so-called uncontaminated family-men are really not masters of themselves. Because they do not look after their family-affairs, they think that they are good and holy men, while, as a matter of fact, they are hen-pecked husbands guided entirely by their wives, and so are but very poor specimens even of common humanity." (27)

HOW'S A FALLEN SANNYASI

Do you know how it looks for a Sannyasi to accept money or to be attached to an object of temptation? It is as if a brahmana widow who had practised continence and lived on simple boiled rice and vegetables and milk for many years, were suddenly to accept an untouchable as her paramour.

There was low-caste woman named Bhagi Teli in our part of the country. She had many disciple and devotees. Finding that she, a sudra, was being saluted by people, the landlord became jealous and engaged a wicked man to tempt her. He succeeded in corrupting her and all her spiritual practice came to nothing. A fallen Sannyasi is like that. (28)

IF YOU WOULD CONQUER LUST, LOOK ON WOMEN AS MOTHER

WHEN asked why he did not lead the life of a householder with his wife, the Master replied: "Kartikeya (Son of Siva) one day happened to scratch a cat with his nail. On going home, he saw that there was the mark of a scratch on the cheek of his Divine Mother, Parvati. Seeing this he asked her, 'Mother, how did you get this ugly scratch on your cheek?' The Mother of the Universe replied, 'This is the work of your own hand; it is the scratch of your nail.' Kartikeya asked in wonder: 'How is it, Mother? I do not remember to have scratched you at any time. The Mother replied, 'Darling, have you forgotten the fact of your having scratched a cat this morning?' Kartikeya said, 'Yes, I did scratch a cat, but how did your cheek get the scar?' The Mother replied, 'Dear child, nothing exists in this world but Myself. The whole creation is Myself; whomsoever you may hurt, you only hurt me.' Kartikeya was greatly surprised to hear this; and then he determined never to marry. For, whom could he marry? Every woman was mother to him. Realizing thus the motherhood of woman, he gave up marriage. I am like Kartikeya. I consider every woman as my Divine Mother." (29)

MONEY IS ALSO A GREAT UPĀDHI

MONEY is also an Upādhi and that too of a very strong nature. As soon as a man becomes rich he is thoroughly changed.

A brahmana who was very meek and humble used to come here[1] every now and then. After sometime he stopped coming and we knew nothing of what had happened to him. One day we went over to Konnagore[2] by boat. As we were getting down from the boat we saw the brahmana sitting on the bank of the Ganges, where, in the fashion of big folks, he was enjoying the pure air of the river. On seeing me he accosted me in a patronising tone with the words, "Hallo Thakur! How are you

1. Refers to Dakshineswar temple garden, where Sri Ramakrishna used to live.
2. A place not very far from Dakshineswar.

doing now?" At once I noticed a change in his tone and said to Hriday who was with me, "I tell you, Hriday, this man must have come by some riches. Can't you see what a great change has come over him?" And Hriday burst into a loud laughter.

The possession of money makes such a difference in a man. (30)

SUCH IS THE PRIDE THAT MONEY BEGETS

A Frog had a rupee, which he kept in his hole. One day an elephant was going over the hole, and the frog coming out in a fit of anger, raised his foot, as if to kick the elephant, and said, "How dare you walk over my head?"

Such is the pride money begets! (31)

Maya

ENMESHED IN MAYA, BRAHMAN WEEPS!

Vishnu incarnated Himself as a sow in order to kill the demon Hiranyaksha. After killing the demon, the sow remained quite happy with her young ones. Forgetting her real nature, she was suckling them very contentedly. The gods in heaven could not persuade Vishnu to relinquish His sow's body and return to the celestial regions. He was absorbed in the happiness of His beast form. After consulting among themselves, the gods sent Siva to the sow. Siva asked the sow, "Why have you forgotten yourself?" Vishnu replied through the sow's body, "Why, I am quite happy here." Thereupon with a stroke of his trident Siva destroyed the sow's body and Vishnu went back to heaven.

Everyone is under the authority of the Divine Mother, Mahamaya, the Primal Energy. Even the Incarnations of God accept the help of Maya to fulfil their mission on earth. Therefore they worship the Primal Energy. (32)

HOW IS MAYA

A CERTAIN sadhu lived for some time in the room above the *nahavat-khana* (concert-room) of the temple of Dakshineswar. He did not speak with anybody and spent his whole time in the meditation of God. One day, all of a sudden, a cloud darkened the sky and shortly afterwards a high wind blew away the cloud. The holy man now came out of his room and began to laugh and dance in the verandah in front of the concert-room. Upon this I asked him, "How is it that you, who spend your days so quietly in your room, are dancing in joy and feel so jolly today?" The holy man replied, "Such is *Maya* that envelops the life!"

At first there is clear sky, all of a sudden a cloud darkens it and presently everything is as before once more. (33)

SUCH INDEED IS MAYA!

ONCE Narada besought the Lord of the universe, "Lord, show me that Maya of Thine which can make the impossible possible." The Lord nodded assent. Subsequently the Lord one day set out on a travel with Narada. After going some distance, He felt very thirsty and fatigued. So He sat down and told Narada, "Narada, I feel very thirsty; please get me a little water from somewhere." Narada at once ran in search of water.

Finding no water nearby, he went far from the place and saw a river at a great distance. When he approached the river, he saw a most charming young lady sitting there, and was at once captivated by her beauty. As soon as Narada went near her, she began to address him in sweet words, and ere long, both fell in love with each other. Narada then married her, and settled down as a house-holder. In course of time he had a number of children by her. And while he was thus living happily with his wife and children, there came a pestilence in the country. Death began to collect its toll from every place. Then Narada proposed to abandon the place and go somewhere else. His wife acceded to it, and they both came out of their house leading their children by the hand. But no sooner did they come to the bridge to cross the river than there came a terrible flood, and in the rush of water, all their children were swept away one after another, and at last the wife too was drowned. Overwhelmed with grief at his bereavement, Narada sat down on the bank and began to weep piteously. Just then the Lord appeared before him, saying. "O Narada, where is the water? And why are you weeping?" The sight of the Lord startled the sage, and then he understood everything. He exclaimed, "Lord, my obeisance to Thee, and my obeisance also to Thy wonderful Maya!" (34)

MAYA VANISHES THE MOMENT IT IS KNOWN

A PRIEST was once going to the village of a disciple of his. He had no servant with him. Seeing a cobbler on the way, he addressed him, saying: "Hullo! good man, will you accompany me as a servant? You will be fed well and taken good care of if you come with me." The cobbler replied: "Sir, I am of the lowest caste. How can I come as your servant?" The priest said, "Never mind. Do not tell anybody what you are. Do not also speak to anyone, or make any body's acquaintance." The cobbler agreed. At twilight, while the priest was sitting at prayers in the house of his disciple, another brahmana came and said to the priest's servant, "Go and bring my shoes from there." True to the behest of his master, he made no response. The brahmana repeated his order a second time, but even then the servant remained silent. The brahmana repeated it again and again, but the cobbler did not move an inch. At last, getting annoyed, the brahmana angrily said: "Sirrah; how dare you disobey a brahmana's command? What is your name? Are you indeed a cobbler?" The cobbler hearing this, began to tremble with fear, and looking piteously at the priest, said: "O venerable sir, I am found out. I dare not stay here any longer. Let me flee." So saying he took to his heels.

Just so, as soon as Maya is recognised, she flies away. (35)

THE PROLONGED DREAM THAT WE CALL LIFE

THERE was a farmer who lived in the country-side. He was a real jnani. He earned his living by farming. He was married, and after many years a son was born to him, whom he named Haru. The parents loved the boy dearly. This was natural, since he was the one precious gem of the family. On account of his religious nature the farmer was loved by the villagers. One day he was working in the field when a neighbour came and told him that Haru had an attack of cholera. The farmer at once returned home and arranged for treatment for the boy. But Haru died. The other members of the family were grief-stricken, but the farmer acted as if nothing had happened. He consoled his family and told them that grieving was futile. Then he went back to his field. On returning home he found his wife weeping even more bitterly. She said to him: "How heartless you are! You haven't shed one tear for the child." The farmer replied quietly: "Shall I tell you why I haven't wept? I had a very vivid dream last night. I dreamt I had become a king; I was the father of eight sons and was very happy with them. Then I woke up. Now I am greatly perplexed. Should I weep for those eight sons or for this one Haru?"

The farmer was a jnani; therefore he realized that the waking state is as unreal as the dream state. There is only one eternal substance, and that is the Atman. (36)

"IT'S NOTHING, IT'S NOTHING"!

It is not easy to get rid of illusion. It lingers even after the attainment of knowledge. A man dreamt of a tiger. Then he woke up and his dream vanished. But his heart continued to palpitate.

Some thieves came to a field. A straw figure resembling a man had been put there to frighten intruders. The thieves were scared by the figure and could not persuade themselves to enter the field. One of them, however, approached and found that it was only a figure made of straw. He came back to his companions and said, "There is nothing to be afraid of." But still they refused to go. They said that their hearts were beating fast. Then the daring thief laid the figure on the ground and said, "It is nothing, it is nothing." This is the process of `Neti, neti.' (37)

IF ALL IS REALLY UNREAL!

RAMA and Lakshmana wanted to go to Ceylon. But the ocean was before them. Lakshmana was angry. Taking his bow and arrow, he said: "I shall kill Varuna. This ocean prevents our going to Ceylon." Rama explained the matter to him, saying: "Lakshmana, all that you are seeing is unreal, like a dream. The ocean is unreal. Your anger is also unreal. It is equally unreal to think of destroying one unreal thing by means of another." (38)

Pitfalls

A SIDDHA STOPS THE STORM

Once a great Siddha was sitting on the sea-shore when there came a great storm. The Siddha, being greatly distressed by it, exclaimed, "let the storm cease!" and his words were fulfilled. Just then a ship was going at a distance with all sails set, and as the wind suddenly died away, it capsized, drowning all who were on board the ship.

Now the sin of causing the death of so many persons accrued to the Siddha, and for this reason he lost all his occult powers and had to suffer in purgatory. (39)

OCCULT POWERS ARE MORE A HINDRANCE THAN A HELP TO GOD-VISION

ONCE upon a time a sadhu acquired great occult powers. He was vain about them. But he was a good man and had some austerities to his credit. One day the Lord, disguised as a holy man, came to him and said, "Revered sir, I have heard that you have great occult powers." The sadhu received the Lord cordially and offered him a seat. Just then an elephant passed by. The Lord, in the disguise of the holy man, said to the sadhu, "Revered sir, can you kill this elephant if you like?" The sadhu said, "Yes, it is possible." So saying he took a pinch of dust, muttered some mantras over it, and threw it at the elephant. The beast struggled a while in pain and then dropped dead. The Lord said: "What power you have! You have killed the elephant!" The sadhu laughed. Again the Lord spoke: "Now, can you revive the elephant?" "That too is possible," replied the sadhu. He threw another pinch of charmed dust at the beast. The elephant writhed about a little and came back to life. Then the Lord said: "Wonderful is your power. But may I ask you one thing? You have killed the elephant and you have revived it. But what has that done for you? Do you feel uplifted by it? Has it enabled you to realize God?" Saying this the Lord vanished.

Subtle are the ways of *Dharma*. One cannot realize God if one has even the least trace of desire. A thread cannot pass through the eye of a needle if it has the smallest fibre sticking out. (40)

THE PANDIT WHO COULD NOT SWIM

ONCE several men were crossing the Ganges in a boat. One of them, a pandit, was making a great display of his erudition, saying that he had studied various books—the Vedas, the Vedanta, and the six systems of philosophy. He asked a fellow passenger, "Do you know the Vedanta?" "No, revered sir." "The Samkhya and the Patanjala?" "No, revered sir." "Have you read no philosophy whatsoever?" "No, revered sir." The pandit was talking in this vain way and the passenger sitting in silence when a great storm arose and the boat was about to sink. The passenger said to the pandit, "Sir, can you swim?" "No", replied the pandit. The passenger said, "I don't know Samkhya or the Patanjala, but I can swim."

What will a man gain by knowing many scriptures? The one thing needful is to know how to cross the river of the world. God alone is real, and all else is illusory. (41)

FOR MAN PROPOSES AND GOD DISPOSES

THE Master (to Pratab Chandra Mazumdar[1]): "You are an educated and intelligent man, and you are a deep thinker too. Keshab and yourself were like two brothers, Gour and Nitai. You have had enough of this world—enough of lectures, controversies, schisms, and the rest. Do you still care for them? Now it is high time for you to collect your scattered mind and turn it towards God. Plunge into the ocean of Divinity."

Mazumdar: "Yes, revered sir, that I ought to do; there is no doubt about it. But all this I do simply to preserve Keshab's name and reputation."

Sri Ramakrishna (smiling): Let me tell you a story. A man built a house on a hill. It was only mud hut, but he had built it with

1. A celebrated Brahmo leader.

great labour. A few days after, there came a violent storm and the hut began to rock. The man became very anxious to save it and prayed to the god of winds:

'O god of the winds, please don't wreck the house!' But the god of the winds paid no heed to his prayers. The house was about to crash. Then he thought of a trick. He remembered that Hanuman was the son of the god of the winds. At once he cried out with great earnestness: 'O revered sir, please don't pull down the house. It belongs to Hanuman. I beseech you to protect it.' But still the house continued to shake violently. Nobody seemed to listen to his prayer. He repeated many times, 'Oh, this house belongs to Hanuman!' But the fury of the winds did not abate. Then he remembered that Hanuman was the devoted servant of Rama, whose younger brother was Lakshmana. Desperately the man cried, saying aloud, 'Oh, this house belongs to Lakshmana!' But that also failed to help matters. So the man cried out as a last resort: 'This is Rama's house. Don't break it down,

O god of winds! I beseech you most humbly.' But this proved futile, and the house began to crash down. Whereupon the man who had to save his own life, rushed out of it with a curse: 'Let it go! This is devil's own house!'

"You may now be anxious to preserve Keshab's name; but console yourself with the thought, it was after all owing to God's Will that the religious movement connected with his name was set on foot, and that if the movement has had its day, it is also due to that same Divine Will. Therefore dive deep into the sea of Immortality." (42)

AS ONE THINKS, SO ONE RECEIVES

A Magician was showing his tricks before a king. Now and then he exclaimed: "Come confusion! Come delusion! O King, give me money! Give me clothes!" Suddenly his tongue turned upward and clove to the roof of his mouth. He experienced kumbhaka. He could utter neither word nor sound, and became motionless. People thought he was dead. They built a vault of bricks and buried him there in that posture. After a thousand years someone dug into the vault. Inside it people found a man seated in samadhi. They took him for a holy man and worshipped him. When they shook him his tongue was loosened and regained its normal position. The magician became conscious of the outer world and cried, as he had a thousand years before: "Come confusion! Come delusion! O King, give me money! Give me clothes!"

God is the Kalpataru, the wish-fulfilling tree. You will certainly get whatever you ask of him. But you must pray standing near the Kalpataru. Only then will your prayer be fulfilled. But you must remember another thing. God knows our inner feeling. A man gets the fulfilment of the desire he cherishes while practising sadhana. As one thinks, so one receives. (43)

'SHE IS SO WELL OFF!'

PEOPLE with little occult power gain such things as name and fame. Many of them want to follow the profession of a guru, gain people's recognition, and make disciples and devotees. Men say of such a guru: "Ah, he is having a wonderful time. How many people visit him! He has many disciples and followers. His house is overflowing with furniture and other things. People give him presents. He has such power that he can feed many people if he so desires."

The profession of a teacher is like that of a prostitute. It is the selling of oneself for the trifle of money, honour, and creature comforts. For such insignificant things it is not good to prostitute the body, mind and soul, the means by which one can attain God. A man said about a certain woman: "Ah! She is having a grand time now. She is so well off! She has rented a room and furnished it with a couch, a mat, pillows, and many other things. And how many people she controls! They are always visiting her." In other words, the woman has now become a prostitute. Therefore her happiness is unbounded! Formerly she was a maid-servant in a gentlemen's house; now she is a prostitute. She has ruined herself for a mere trifle. (44)

FEIGNING MADNESS TOO IS RISKY!

A CERTAIN person, deeply involved in debt, feigned madness to escape the consequences of his liabilities. Physicians failed to cure his disease, and the more he was treated for his ailments the greater became his madness. At last a wise physician found out the truth, and, taking the feigning mad man aside, rebuked him saying: "My friend, what are you doing? Beware lest in feigning madness you become really mad. Already you have developed some genuine signs of insanity." This sensible advice awoke the man from his folly, and he left off acting the part of a mad man.

By constantly acting a thing, one actually becomes that. (45)

WELCOME GOOD, AND EVIL WELCOMES YOU

A BRAHMANA was laying out a garden. He looked after it day and night. One day a cow strayed into the garden and browsed on a mango sapling of which the brahmana used to take special care. When he saw the cow destroying his favourite plant, the brahmana became wild with rage, and gave such a severe beating to the animal that it died of the injuries received. The news soon spread like wild-fire that the brahmana had killed the sacred animal. When any one attributed the sin of that act to him, the brahmana, who professed himself to be a Vedantin, denied the charge, saying: "No, I have not killed the cow; it is my hand that had done it; and as god Indra is the presiding deity of the hand, it is he who has incurred the sin of killing the cow, not I." Indra, in his heaven, heard of this. He assumed the shape of an old brahmana, and coming to the owner of the garden, said, "Sir, whose garden is this?"

Brahmana: Mine

Indra: It is a beautiful garden. You have got a skilful gardener; for see how neatly and artistically he has planted the trees.

Brahmana: Well, sir, that is all my work. The trees were planted under my personal supervision and direction.

Indra: Very nicely done, indeed! Who has laid out this path? It is very well-planned and neatly executed.

Brahmana: All that has been done by me.

Then Indra said with folded hands, "When all these things are yours, and when you take credit for all the work done in this garden, it is not proper that poor Indra should be made responsible for killing the cow." (46)

WHAT OCCULT POWERS ARE LIKE

HRIDAY asked me—I was then under his control—to pray to the Divine Mother for (occult) powers. I went to the temple. In a vision I saw a widow thirty or thirtyfive years old, covered with filth. It was revealed to me that occult powers are like that filth.

I became angry with Hriday because he had asked me to pray for powers. (47)

'HORSES IN COWSHED!'

THE instruction of a man who has not seen God does not produce the right effect. He may say one thing rightly, but he becomes confused about the next.

Samadhyayi[1] delivered a lecture. He said, "God is beyond words and mind; He is dry. Worship Him through the bliss of your love and devotion." Just see, he thus described God, Whose very nature is Joy and Bliss! What will such a lecture accomplish? Can it teach people anything? Such a lecturer is like the man who said, "My uncle's cowshed is full of horses." Horses in cowshed! From that you understand that there were no horses at all.

(. . . . Nor cows either!) (48)

THOSE FASCINATING OBSTRUCTIONS

ADDRESSING a devotee named Mahendra Mukherjee, said Sri Ramakrishna: "You have no children. You do not serve anybody. And still you have no leisure! Goodness gracious!"

"You have no children to divert your mind. I know a deputy magistrate who draws a salary of eight hundred rupees a month. He went to Keshab's house to see a performance.

---

1. A leader of the Brahmo Samaj.

I was there too. Rakhal[1] and a few other devotees were with me and sat beside me. After a while Rakhal went out for a few minutes. The deputy magistrate came over and made his young son take Rakhal's seat. I said, 'He can't sit there.' At that time I was in such a state of mind that I had to do whatever the person next to me would ask me to do; so I had seated Rakhal beside me. As long as the performance lasted the deputy did nothing but gibber with his son. The rascal didn't look at the performance even once. I heard, too, that he is a slave to his wife; he gets up and sits down as she tells him to. And he didn't see the performance for that snubnosed monkey of a boy." (49)

1. Later known as Swami Brahmananda, the first president of the Ramakrishna Order.

Egotism : Vanity

FROM 'HAMBA' TO 'TUHU'

The cow cries 'Hamba!', which means 'I'. That is why it suffers so much. It is yoked to the plough and made to work in rain and sun. Then it may be killed by the butcher. From its hide shoes are made, and also drums, which are mercilessly beaten. Still it does not escape suffering. At last strings are made out of its entrails for the bows used in carding cotton. Then it no longer says, 'Hamba! Hamba!', 'I! I!', but 'Tuhu! Tuhu!', 'Thou! Thou!' Only then are its troubles over.

O Lord, I am the servant; Thou art the Master. I am the child; Thou art the Mother.

Egotism is the cause of all suffering. (50)

EGOTISM IS RUINOUS

A DISCIPLE who had firm faith in the infinite power of his Guru walked over the river by simply uttering his name. Seeing this, the Guru thought, "Well, is there such a power in my mere name? Then how great and powerful must I be!" The next day, the Guru also tried to walk over the river uttering 'I', 'I', 'I', but no sooner did he step into the water than he sank down and was soon drowned; for the poor man did not know how to swim even.

Faith can achieve miracles while vanity or egotism brings about the destruction of man. (51)

SANKARACHARYA AND HIS FOOLISH DISCIPLE

THE great Sankaracharya had a foolish disciple who used to imitate his Master in all matters. Sankara uttered *'Sivoham'* (I am Siva); the disciple also repeated *'Sivoham'*. To correct his disciple's folly, Sankara one day, while passing by a smithy, took a potful of molten iron and swallowed it; and he asked that disciple also to do the same. Of course, the disciple could not imitate this act of his Master, and thence forward he left off saying *'Sivoham'*. (52)

WHEN SIVA'S BULL BARED ITS TEETH—

GOD alone is the Doer, and we are all His instruments. Therefore it is impossible even for a Jnani to be egotistic. The writer of a hymn to Siva felt proud of his achievement; but his pride was dashed to pieces when Siva's bull bared his teeth. He saw that each tooth was a word of the hymn.

Do you understand the meaning of this? These words had existed from the beginningless past. The writer had only discovered them. (53)

HOW VANITY TURNS A PERSON'S HEAD!

THOSE who have read a few books cannot get rid of conceit. Once I had a talk with Kalikrishna Tagore about God. At once he said, "I know all about that." I said to him: "Does a man who had visited Delhi brag about that? Does a gentleman go about telling everyone that he is a gentleman?"

Oh, how vanity turns a person's head! There was a scavenger woman in the temple garden at Dakshineswar. And her pride! And all for a few ornaments. One day a few men were passing her on the path and she shouted to them, “Hey! get out of the way, you people!” If a scavenger women could talk that way, what can one say about the vanity of others? (54)

Previous Tendencies

POWERFUL ARE THE INBORN TENDENCIES

Let me tell you how powerful inborn tendencies are. A prince had, in a previ ous birth, been the son of a washerman. While playing with his chums in his incarnation as the prince, he said to them: "Stop those games, I shall show you a new one. I shall lie on my belly, and you will beat the clothes on my back as the washerman does, making swishing sound." (55)

A HINDU WHO WAS FORCED TO EMBRACE ISLAM

ONCE there lived a very pious HIndu who always worshipped the Divine Mother and chanted Her name. When the Mussalmans conquered the country, they forced him to embrace Islam. They said to him: "You are now a Mussalman. Say 'Allah'. From now on you must repeat only the name of 'Allah.'" With great difficulty he repeated the word

'Allah', but every now and then blurted out 'Jagadamba'. At that the Mussalmans were about to beat him. Thereupon he said to them: `I beseech you! Please do not kill me. I have been trying my utmost to repeat the name of Allah, but our Jagadamba has filled me up to the throat. She pushes out your Allah".

It is not an easy thing to destroy old tendencies. (56)

NOTHING IS LOST IN THE ECONOMY OF GOD

THERE is a story about a man who practised Sava-sadhana[1]. He worshipped the Divine Mother in a deep forest. First he saw many terrible visions. Finally a tiger attacked and killed him. Another man, happening to pass by and seeing the approach of the tiger, had climbed a tree. Afterwards he got down and found all the arrangements for worship at hand. He performed some purifying ceremonies and seated himself on the corpse.

1. A religious practice prescribed by the Tantras, in which the aspirant uses a Sava, or corpse, as his seat for meditation.

No sooner had he done a little Japa than the Divine Mother appeared before him and said: "My child, I am very much pleased with you. Accept a boon from Me." He bowed low at the Lotus Feet of the Goddess and said: "May I ask you one question, Mother? I am speechless with amazement at your action. The other man worked so hard to get the ingredients for Your worship and tried to propitiate You for such a long time, but You did not condescend to show him Your favour. And I, who don't know anything of worship, who have done nothing, who have neither devotion nor knowledge nor love, and who haven't practised any austerities, am receiving so much of Your grace?" The Divine Mother said with a smile, "My child, you don't remember your previous births. For many births you tried to propitiate Me through austerities. As a result of those austerities all these things have come to hand, and you have been blessed with My vision. Now ask me your boon."

One must admit the existence of tendencies inherited from previous births. (57)

THE INEVITABLES

EVERYONE must reap the result of his past Karma. One must admit the influence of tendencies inherited from the past births and the result of the *prārabdha karma*. . . .And one must remember that pleasure and pain are the characteristics of the embodied state. In Kavi Kankan's *Chandi* it is written that Kaluvir was sent to prison and a heavy stone placed on his chest. Yet Kalu was born as the result of a boon from the Divine Mother of the Universe. Thus pleasure and pain are inevitable when one accepts a body. Again, take the case of Srimanta, who was a great devotee. Though his mother, Khullana, was very much devoted to the Divine Mother, there was no end to his troubles. He was almost beheaded. There is also the instance of the wood-cutter who was a great lover of the Divine Mother. She appeared before him and showed him much grace and love; but he had to continue his profession of wood-cutting, and earn his livelihood by that arduous work. Again, while Devaki, Krishna's Mother, was in the prison she had a vision of God Himself endowed with four hands, holding mace, discus, conch-shell and lotus. But with all that she could not get out of the prison. (58)

The Way

THE ONLY WAY

Why shouldn't one be able to lead a spiritual life in the world? But it is extremely difficult.

Once I passed over the bridge at Baghbazar[1]. How many chains it is tied with! Nothing will happen if one chain is broken, for there are so many others to keep it in place. Just so there are many ties on a worldly man. There is no way for him to get rid of them except through the grace of God. (59)

---

1. In Calcutta.

Faith

THIS FAITH OF A CHILD

A boy named Jatila used to walk to school through the woods, and the journey frightened him. One day he told his mother of his fear. She replied: "Why should you be afraid? Call Madhusudana." "Mother," asked the boy, "Who is Madhusudana?" The mother said, "He is your Elder Brother." One day after this, when the boy again felt afraid in the woods, he cried out, "O Brother Madhu sudana!" But there was no response. He began to weep aloud: "Where are You, Brother Madhusudana? Come to me. I am afraid." Then God could no longer stay away. He appeared before the boy and said: "Here I am. Why are you frightened?" And so saying He took the boy out of the woods and showed him the way to school. When He took leave of the boy, God said: "I will come whenever you call me. Do not be afraid."

One must have this faith of a child, this yearning. (60)

A BOY ACTUALLY FED GOD

A BRAHMAN used to worship his family Deity with food offerings. One day he had to go away on business. As he was about to leave the house, he said to his son: "Give the offering to the Deity today. See that God is fed." The boy offered food in the shrine, but the image remained silent on the altar. It would neither eat nor talk. The boy waited a long time, but still the image did not move. But the boy firmly believed that God would come down from His throne, sit on the floor, and partake of his food. Again and again he prayed to the Deity, saying: "O Lord, come down and eat the food. It is already very late. I cannot sit here any longer." But the image did not utter a word. The boy burst into tears and cried: "O Lord, my father asked me to feed you. Why won't you come down? Why won't you eat from my hands?" The boy wept for some time with a longing soul. At last the Deity, smiling, came down from the altar and sat before the meal and ate it. After feeding the Deity, the boy came out of the shrine room. His relative said: "The worship is over. Now bring away the offering." "Yes," said the boy, "the worship is over. But God has eaten everything." "How is that?" asked the relatives. The boy replied innocently, "Why, God has eaten the food." They entered the shrine and were speechless with wonder to see that the Deity had really eaten every bit of the offering. (61)

A DISCIPLE AND HER POT OF CURDS

ONCE there was an *annaprāsana*[1] ceremony is a Guru's house. His disciples volunteered, according to their powers, to supply the different articles of food. He had one disciple, a very poor widow, who owned a cow. She milked it and brought the Guru a jar of milk. He had thought she would take charge of all the milk and curd for the festival. Angry at her poor offering, he threw the milk away and said to

1. A Hindu religious ceremony in connection with the first offering of cooked rice to a baby.

her, "Go and drown yourself." The widow accepted this as his command and went to the river to drown herself. But God was pleased with her guileless faith and, appearing before her, said: "Take this pot of curd. You will never be able to empty it. The more curd you pour out, the more will come from the pot. This will satisfy your teacher." The Guru was speechless with amazement when the pot was given to him. After hearing from the widow the story of the pot, he went to the river, saying to her, "I shall drown myself if you cannot show God to me." God appeared then and there, but the Guru could not see Him. Addressing God, the widow said, "If my teacher gives up his body because Thou dost not reveal Thyself to Him, then I too shall die." So God appeared to the Guru—but only once. (62)

THE SIMPLE SECRET

GOD can be realised through child-like faith and guilelessness.

A certain person, on coming across a sadhu, humbly begged him for instruction.

The sadhu's advice was, "Love God with all your heart and soul." The enquirer replied, "I have never seen God, nor do I know anything about Him; how is it possible that I should love Him?" The holy man enquired whom the other loved most. The answer was, "I have nobody to care for. I have a sheep and that is the only creature I love." The sadhu said: "Then tend the creature and love it with all your heart and soul, and always remember that the Lord abides in it." Having given this advice the sadhu left the place. The enquirer now began to tend the sheep with loving care, fully believing that the Lord abode in the creature. After a long time the sadhu, during his return journey, sought out the person he had advised and enquired how he was getting on. The latter saluted the sadhu and said, "Master, I am all right, thanks to your kind instructions. Much good has come to me by following the line of thought prescribed by you. Time and again I see a beautiful figure with four hands within my sheep and I find supreme bliss in that." (63)

THE BASIC FAITH

A MAN must have some kind of faith before he undertakes a work. Further, he feels joy when he thinks of it. Only then does he set about performing the work. Suppose a jar of gold coins is hidden under-ground. First of all a man must have faith that the jar of gold coins is there. He feels joy at the thought of the jar. Then he begins to dig. As he removes the earth he hears a metallic sound. That increases his joy. Next he sees a corner of the jar. That gives him more joy. Thus his joy is ever on the increase.

Standing on the porch of the Kali temple, I have watched the ascetics preparing their smoke of hemp. I have seen their face beaming with joy in anticipation of the smoke. (64)

A TRUE DEVOTEE'S FAITH

ONCE, while going to Kamarpukur, I was overtaken by a storm. I was in the middle of a big meadow. The place was haunted by robbers. I began to repeat the names of all the deities: Rama, Krishna and Bhagavathi. I also repeated the name of Hanuman. I chanted the names of them all.

What does that mean? Let me tell you. While the servant is counting out the money to purchase supplies, he says, "These pennies for potatoes, these for egg-plants, these for fish." He counts the money separately, but after the list is completed, he puts the coins together.

Is there anything impossible for faith? And a true devotee has faith in everything: the formless Reality, God with form, Rama, Krishna and the Divine Mother. (65)

FAITH ABSOLUTE

ONCE a young sannyasin went to a house to beg his meal. He had embraced the monastic life from his very boyhood and so had not much knowledge of the world. A young lady came out from the house to give him alms. Seeing her breasts, the young sannyasin questioned her if she was suffering from boils on her chest. To that her mother replied: "No, my son, she hasn't got any boil. A child will soon be born to her, and so God has provided her with two breasts to suckle the child. The child will suck milk from those breasts after it is born." No sooner did the young sannyasin hear this than he exclaimed: "No more will I beg my meals. He who has created me, will feed me too." (66)

FAITH UNBOUNDED

ONE day, Sri Krishna, while going in a chariot along with Arjuna, looked up to the sky and said, "Behold! What a nice flight of pigeons there!" Arjuna at once turned his eyes in that direction and exclaimed, "Really, friend, very beautiful pigeons indeed!" But the very next moment Sri Krishna looked again and said, "No, friend, they are not pigeons, it seems." Arjuna, too, saw again and said, "True, they are not pigeons."

Now try to understand the meaning of this. A great adherent to truth that Arjuna was, he did not possibly assent to whatever Sri Krishna said, simply for flattering him. But he had such an unflinching faith in Sri Krishna that he perceived at once actually whatever Sri Krishna said.

FAITH TREMENDOUS

If a devotee believes one hundred per cent that his Chosen Ideal is God, then he attains God and sees Him.

People of bygone generations had tremendous faith. What faith Haladhari's[1] father had! Once he was on the way to his daughter's house when he noticed some beautiful flowers and bel leaves. He gathered them for the worship of the family Deity and walked back five or six miles to his own house.

Once a theatrical troupe in the village was enacting the life of Rama. When Kaikeyi asked Rama to go into exile in the forest, Haladhari's father, who had been watching the performance, sprang up. He went to the actor who played Kaikeyi, crying out, "You wretch!", and was about to burn the actor's face with a torch.

He was a very pious man. After finishing his ablutions he would stand in the water

1. A priest in the temple garden at Dakshineswar and a cousin of Sri Ramakrishna.

and meditate on the Deity, reciting the invocation: "I meditate on Thee, of red hue and four faces," while tears streamed down his cheeks. (68)

THE POWER OF FAITH

You must have heard about the tremendous power of faith. It is said in the Purana that Rama, who was God Himself—the embodiment of Absolute Brahman—had to build a bridge to cross the sea to Ceylon. But Hanuman, trusting in Rama's name, cleared the sea in one jump and reached the other side. He had no need of a bridge. (69)

HANUMAN SINGH AND THE WRESTLER FROM THE PUNJAB

At one time two men were engaged to wrestle. One of them was Hanuman Singh and the other a Mussalman from the Punjab. The Mussalman was a strong and stout man. He had eaten lustily of butter and meat for fifteen days before the day of the wrestling-match, and even on that day. All thought he would be the victor. Hanuman Singh, on the other hand, clad in dirty cloth, had eaten sparingly for some days before the day of the match and devoted himself to repeating the holy name of Mahavir.[1] On the day of the match he observed a complete fast. All thought he would surely be defeated. But it was he who won, while the man who had feasted for fifteen days lost the fight. (70)

FAITH KNOWS NO MIRACLES

ONCE there lived two yogis who were practising austerities with a view to realize the Lord. One day Narada, the divine sage, was passing by their hermitage, when one of them asked him, "Are you coming from Heaven?" Narada replied, "Yes, that is so." The yogi said, "Do tell me what you saw the Lord doing in Heaven." Narada replied, "I saw the Lord playing by making camels and elephants pass through the eye of a needle." At this the yogi observed: "There is nothing in it to marvel at. Nothing

1. Mahavir, or Hanuman, is the patron deity of wrestlers.

is impossible with God!" But the other man exclaimed: "O nonsense! That is impossible! It only shows that you have never been to the Lord's abode." The first man was bhakta and had the faith of a child. Nothing is impossible to the Lord, nor can any one know His nature fully. Everything can be predicted of Him. (71)

BUT FAITH WORKS MIRACLES

ONCE the son of a certain man lay at the point of death, and it seemed that none could save his life. A sadhu, however, said to the father of the dying son: "There is but one hope. If you can get in a human skull the venom of a cobra mixed with a few drops of rain-water under the constellation of the Svati star, your son's life can be saved." The father looked up the almanac and found that the constellation of the Svati would be in the ascendant on the morrow. So he prayed, saying, "O Lord, do Thou make possible all these conditions, and spare the life of my son." With extreme earnestness and longing in his heart, he set out on the following evening and diligently sear-ched in a deserted spot for a human skull. At last he found one under a tree, held it in the hand, and waited for the rain, praying. Suddenly a shower came, and a few drops of rain were deposited in the upturned skull. The man said to himself, "Now I have the water in the skull under the right constellation." Then he prayed earnestly, "Grant, O Lord, that the rest may also be obtained." In a short time he discovered, not far from there, a toad, and a cobra springing to catch it. In a moment the toad jumped over the skull, followed by the cobra whose venom fell into the skull. With overwhelming gratitude the anxious father cried out: "Lord, by Thy grace even impossible things are made possible. Now I know that my son's life will be saved."

Therefore, I say, if you have true faith and earnest longing, you will get everything by the grace of the Lord. (72)

FAITH IS THE MOTHER OF MIRACLES

A MILK-MAID used to supply milk to a brahmana priest living on the other side of a river.

Owing to the irregularities of the boat service, she could not supply him milk punctually every day. Once, being rebuked for her going late, the poor woman said, "What can I do? I start early from my house, but have to wait for a long time at the river bank for the boatman and the passengers." The priest said, "Woman! They cross the ocean of life by uttering the name of God, and can't you cross this little river?" The simple-hearted woman became very glad at heart on learning this easy means of crossing the river. From the next day the milk was being supplied early in the morning. One day the priest said to the woman, "How is it that you are no longer late nowadays?" She said, "I cross the river by uttering the name of the Lord as you told me to do, and don't stand now in need of a boatman." The priest could not believe this and said, "Can you show me how you cross the river?" The woman took him with her and began to walk over the water. Looking behind, the woman saw the priest in a sad plight and said, "How is it, sir, that you are uttering the name of God with your mouth, but at the same time with your hands you are trying to keep your cloth untouched by water? You do not fully rely on Him."

Entire resignation and absolute faith in God are at the root of all miraculous deeds. (73)

POWER OF THE HOLY NAME

A KING who was guilty of the heinous sin of killing a brahmana went to the hermitage of a Rishi to learn what penance he must perform in order to be purified. The Rishi was absent, but his son was in the hermitage. Hearing the problem of the king, he said, "Repeat the 'name' of God (Rama) three times, and your sin will be expiated." When the Rishi came back and heard of the penance prescribed by his son, he remarked indignantly, "Sins committed in myriads of births are purged immediately by uttering the 'name' of the Almighty but once. How weak must be your faith, O fool, since you have ordered the holy 'name' to be repeated thrice? For this weakness of your faith, you shall become an out-caste." And the son became Guhaka of the Ramayana. (74)

THE DOUBTING SOUL PERISHES

ONCE a man was about to cross the sea. Vibhishana wrote Rama's name on a leaf, tied it in a corner of the man's wearing cloth, and said to him: "Don't be afraid. Have faith and walk on the water. But look here—the moment you lose faith you will be drowned." The man was walking easily on the water. Suddenly he had an intense desire to see what was tied in his cloth. He opened it and found only a leaf with the name of Rama written on it. "What is this?" he thought. "Just the name of Rama!" As soon as doubt entered his mind he sank under the water. (75)

Devotion

THE BEST OFFERING TO GOD IS LOVE

Once a servant of a rich man came to his master's house, and stood in a corner with great reverence and humility. He held in his hand something covered with a cloth. The Master enquired, "What is there in your hand?" The servant brought out a small custard-apple from beneath the cloth and kept it humbly before the master, feeling that he would be much gratified if the master would take it. The master was much pleased to see the loving devotion of the servant and accepted the offering, though a trifle. With great delight he exclaimed: "Ah, what a fine fruit is this! Where did you get it from?"

In the same way God looks into the heart of the devotee. He is infinite in His grandeur, yet He is responsive to the influence of love and devotion. (76)

THE LOVE THAT FREELY GIVETH IS THE HIGHEST

PRIDE once entered into the heart of Arjuna, the beloved friend of Sri Krishna. Arjuna thought that none equalled him in love and devotion to his Lord and Friend. The omniscient Lord, Sri Krishna, reading the heart of His friend, took him one day for a walk. They had not proceeded far when Arjuna saw a strange brahmana eating dry grass as food, but nevertheless had a sword dangling at his side. Arjuna at once knew him to be a holy and pious devotee of Vishnu, one whose highest religious duty was to injure no being. As even grass has life, he would not eat it green but sustained his life by eating it dry and lifeless. Yet he carried a sword. Arjuna, wondering at the incongruity, turned towards the Lord and said: "How is this? Here is a man who has re-nounced all ideas of injuring any living being, down to the meanest blade of grass; yet he carries with him a sword, the symbol of death and hatred!" The Lord said, "You had better ask the man yourself". Arjuna then went up to the brahmana and said: "Sir, you injure no living being, and you live upon dry grass. Why then do you carry this sharp sword?"

The brahmana: It is to punish four persons if I chance to meet them.

Arjuna: Who are they?

The brahmana: The first is the wretch Narada.

Arjuna: Why, what has he done?

The brahmana: Why, look at the audacity of that fellow; he is perpetually keeping my Lord awake with his songs and music. He has no consideration whatsoever for the comfort of the Lord. Day and night, in and out of season, he disturbs the peace of the Lord by his prayers and praises.

Arjuna: Who is the second person?

The brahmana: The impudent Draupadi.

Arjuna: What is her fault?

The brahmana: Look at the inconsiderate audacity of the woman! She was so rash as to call my beloved Lord just at the moment He was going to dine. He had to give up His dinner and go to the Kamyaka Vana to save the Pandavas from the curse of Durvasa. And her presumption went so far that she even caused my beloved Lord to eat the impure remnant of her own food.

Arjuna: Who is the third?

The brahmana: It is the heartless Prahlada. He was so cruel that he did not hesitate for a moment to ask my Lord to enter the boiling cauldron of oil, to be trodden under the heavy feet of the elephants and to break through an adamantine pillar.

Arjuna: Who is the fourth?

The brahmana: The wretch Arjuna.

Arjuna: Why, what fault has he committed?

The brahmana: Look at his felony. He made my beloved Lord take the mean office of a charioteer of his car in the great war of Kurukshetra.

Arjuna was amazed at the depth of the poor brahmana's devotion and love, and from that moment his pride vanished, and he gave up thinking that he was the best devotee of the Lord. (77)

WHO WINS THE PRIZE

KARTIKA and Ganesa[1] were seated near Bhagavati, who had a necklace of gems around Her neck. The Divine Mother said to them, "I will present this necklace to him who is the first to go around the universe." Thereupon Kartika, without losing a moment, set out on the peacock, his carrier. Ganesa, on the other hand, in a leisurely fashion went around the Divine Mother and prostrated himself before Her. He knew that She contained within Herself the entire universe. The Divine Mother was pleased with him and put the necklace around his neck. After a long while Kartika returned and found his brother seated there with the necklace on.

Everything can be realised simply through love of God. If one is able to love God, one does not lack anything. (78)

THAT GREAT DEVOTEE OF A CROW

RAMA and Lakshmana visited Pampa Lake. Lakshmana saw a crow very eager for water.

1. The two sons of Bhagavati, the Divine Mother.

Again an again it went to the edge of the water but would not drink. Lakshmana asked Rama about it. Rama said: "Brother, this crow is a great devotee of God. Day and night it repeats the name of Rama. Its throat is parched with thirst, but still it won't drink for fear of missing a repetition of Rama's name." (79)

THREE FRIENDS AND THE TIGER

ONCE three friends were going through a forest, when a tiger suddenly appeared before them. "Brothers," one of them exclaimed, "we are lost!" "Why should you say that?" said the second friend, "Why should we be lost? Come, let us pray to God." The third friend said: "No. Why should we trouble God about it? Come, let us climb this tree."

The friend who said 'We are lost!' did not know that there is a God who is our Protector. The friend who asked the others to pray to God was a jnani. He was aware that God is the Creator, Preserver and Destroyer of the world. The third friend, who didn't want to trouble God with prayers and suggested climbing the tree, had ecstatic love of God. It is the very nature of such love that it makes a man think himself stronger than his Beloved. He is always alert lest his Beloved should suffer. The one desire of his is to keep his Beloved from even being pricked in the foot by a thorn. (80)

SINGLE-MINDED DEVOTION TO ONE IDEAL

ONCE the Pandava brothers performed the Rajasuya sacrifice. All the kings placed Yudhisthira on the royal throne and bowed low before him in homage. But Vibhishana, the king of Ceylon, said, 'I bow down to Narayana and none else." At these words the Lord Krishna bowed down to Yudhisthira. Only then did Vibhishana prostrate himself, crown and all, before him.

Such is unswerving and single-minded devotion to one ideal. (81)

IN WEAL AND WOE, GOD FOR EVERMORE

IN a certain village there lived a weaver. He was a very pious soul. Everyone trusted him and loved him. He used to sell his goods in the market-place. When a customer asked him the price of a cloth, the weaver would say: "By the will of Rama the price of the yarn is one rupee and the labour four annas; by the will of Rama the profit is two annas. The price of the cloth, by the will of Rama, is one rupee and six annas." Such was the people's faith in the weaver that the customer would at once pay the price and take the cloth. The weaver was a real devotee of God. After finishing his supper in the evening, he would spend long hours in the worship hall meditating on God and chanting His name and glories. Now, late one night the weaver couldn't sleep. He was sitting in the worship hall, smoking, now and then, when a band of robbers happened to pass that way. They wanted a man to carry their goods and said to the weaver, "Come with us." So saying, they led him off by the hand. After committing a robbery in a house, they put a load of things on the weaver's head commanding him to carry them. Suddenly the police arrived and the robbers ran away. But the weaver, with his load, was arrested. He was kept in the lock-up for the night. Next day he was brought before the magistrate for trial. The villagers learnt what had happened and came to the court. They said to the magistrate, "Your Honour, this man could never commit robbery." Thereupon the magistrate asked the weaver to make his statement.

The weaver said: "Your Honour, by the will of Rama I finished my meal at night. Then by the will of Rama I was sitting in the worship hall. It was quite late at night by the will of Rama. By the will of Rama I had been thinking of God and chanting His name and glories, when by the will of Rama a band of robbers passed that way. By the will of Rama they dragged me with them; by the will of Rama they committed a robbery in a house; and by the will of Rama they put a load on my head. Just then, by the will of Rama the police arrived and by the will of Rama I was arrested. Then by the will of Rama the police kept me in the lock-up for the night, and this morning by the will of Rama I have been brought before Your Honour." The magistrate realized that the weaver was a pious man and ordered his release. On his way home the weaver said to his friends, "By the will of Rama I have been released."

Whether you live in the world or renounce it, everything depends upon the will of Rama. Throwing your whole responsibility upon God, do your work in the world. (82)

RAVANA—THE GREAT DEVOTEE OF RAMA

MANDODARI told her royal husband Ravana, "If you are so intent upon having Sita as your queen, why don't you impose on her by assuming the form of her husband Rama with the help of your magical powers?" "Fie on you!" exclaimed Ravana "Can I stoop to the pleasures of the sense while I am in the holy form of Rama—a form the very thought of which fills my heart with such unspeakable joy and blessedness that even the highest heaven appears to me worthless?" (83)

DEVOTION, THE DIVINE OPEN SESAME

HAVING received no news of her Gopala (Krishna, God incarnate), Yasoda once came to Radha and asked her if she had any news from Him. At that time Radha was in a deep trance, and so did not hear Yasoda. Subsequently, when her trance was over, she saw Yasoda, the queen of Nanda, sitting before her. Bowing down to her at once, Radha asked Yasoda the reason of her visit, and when Yasoda stated the reason, she said: "Mother, shut your eyes and meditate upon the form of Gopala, and you will be able to see Him." And as soon as Yasoda shut her eyes, Radha, who was herself the very essence of spiritual feelings (Bhāva), overwhelmed her with her power, and in that superconscious mood, Yasoda saw her Gopala. Then Yasoda asked this boon of Radha, "Mother, grant me that I may see my beloved Gopala whenever I close my eyes." (84)

A DEVOTEE AVOIDS WHAT THE WORLD RUNS AFTER

AFTER the death of Ravana, his brother Vibhishana refused to be the King of Ceylon. He said: "O Rama, I have obtained you. What shall I do with Kingship?" Rama said: "Vibhishana, be King for the sake of the ignorant, for those who might ask what riches you have gained by serving me so much. Be King to give them a lesson." (85)

'GLORY UNTO KRISHNA!'

ONCE I went to a certain place with Mathur Babu. Many pundits came forward to argue with me. And you know that I am a fool. The pundits saw that strange mood of mine.

When the conversation was over, they said to me: "Sir, after hearing your words, all that we have studied before, our knowledge and scholarship, has proved to be mere spittle. Now we realize that a man does not lack wisdom if he has the grace of God." 'The fool becomes wise and the mute eloquent.' Therefore I say that a man does not become a scholar by the mere study of books.

Yes, how true it is! How can a man who has the grace of God lack knowledge? Look at me. I am a fool. I do not know anything. Then who is it that utters these words?

The reservoir of knowledge of God is inexhaustible. There are grain dealers at Kamarpukur. When selling paddy, one man weighs the grain on the scales and another man pushes it to him from a heap. It is the duty of the second man to keep a constant supply of grain on the scales by pushing it from the big heap. It is the same with my words. No sooner are they about to run short than the Divine Mother sends a new supply from Her inexhaustible storehouse of knowledge.

You know I am a fool. I know nothing. Then who is it that says all these things?... Her's (Divine Mother's) is the glory; we are only Her instruments. Once Radha, to prove her chastity, carried on her head a pitcher filled with water. The pitcher had a thousand holes, but not a drop of water spilled. People began to praise her, saying, "Such a chaste woman the world will never see again!" Then Radha said to them: "Why do you praise me? Say, 'Glory unto Krishna! Hail Krishna!' I am only His handmaid." (86)

THAT PURE LOVE FOR GOD

IN the course of his pilgrimage through the southern parts of India, Sri Chaitanya Deva came across a certain devotee who was in tears all the while a pundit was reading from the Gita. Now this devotee knew not even a single word of the Gita. On being asked why he shed tears, he replied, "It is indeed true that I do not know a word of the Gita. But all the while it was being read, I could not help seeing with my inner eye the beautiful form of my Lord Sri Krishna seated before Arjuna in a chariot in the field of Kurukshetra, and giving out all those sublime thoughts embodied in the Gita. This it was that filled my eyes with tears of joy and love."

This man who knew not letters, had the highest Knowledge, for he had pure love for God and could realize Him. (87)

BACK TO THE DIVINE MOTHER

A DEVOTEE who is born with an element of Vishnu cannot altogether get rid of bhakti.

Once I fell into the clutches of a Jnani, who made me listen to Vedanta for eleven months. But he could not altogether destroy the seed of bhakti in me. No matter where my mind wandered, it would come back to the Divine Mother. Whenever I sang to Her, Nangta[1] would weep and say, 'Ah! what is this?' You see, he was such a great Jnani and still he wept. Remember the popular saying that if a man drinks the juice of the alekh creeper, a plant grows inside his stomach.

Once the seed of Bhakti is sown, the effect is inevitable; it will gradually grow into a tree with flowers and fruits.

You may reason and argue a thousand times, but if you have the seed of bhakti within you, you will surely come back to Hari. (88)

CONCEIT IS TO DEVOTION WHAT CANKER IS TO BUDS

ONCE upon a time conceit entered into the heart of Narada, and he thought there was

1. The Master here speaks of Totapuri, the monk who initiated him into the practice of non-dual Vedanta. Him Sri Ramakrishna always refers to as "Nangta," or the "naked one."

no greater devotee than himself. Reading his heart, the Lord said: “Narada, go to such and such a place. A great devotee of mine is living there. Cultivate his acquaintance; for he is truly devoted to Me.” Narada went there and found an agriculturist who rose early in the morning, pronounced the name of Hari (God) only once, and taking his plough, went out and tilled the ground all day long. At night he went to bed after pronouncing the name of Hari once more. Narada said to himself: “how can this rustic be a lover of God? I see him busily engaged in wordly duties, and he has no signs of a pious man about him.” Then Narada went back to the Lord and spoke what he thought of his new acquaintance. Thereupon the Lord said: “Narada, take this cup of oil and go round this city and come back with it. But take care that you do not spill even a single drop of it.” Narada did as he was told, and on his return the Lord asked him, “Well, Narada, how many times did you remember Me in the course of your walk round the city?” “Not once, my Lord,” said Narada, “and how could

I, when I had to watch this cup brimming over with oil?" The Lord then said: "This one cup of oil did so divert your attention that even you did forget Me altogether. But look at that rustic, who, though carrying the heavy burden of a family, still remembers Me twice every day." (89)

GOD ALONE IS THE GIVER

WHEN Akbar was the Emperor of Delhi there lived a hermit in a hut in the forest. Many people visited the holy man. At one time he felt a great desire to entertain his visitors. But how could he do so without money? So he decided to go to the Emperor for help, for the gate of Akbar's palace was always open to holy men. The hermit entered the palace while the Emperor was at his daily devotions and took a seat in a corner of the room. He heard the Emperor conclude his worship with the prayer, "O God, give me money; give me riches", and so on and so forth. When the hermit heard this he was about to leave the prayer hall, but the Emperor signed to him to wait. When the prayer was over the Emperor said to him, "You came to see me; how is it that you were about to leave without saying anything to me?" "Your Majesty need not trouble yourself about it", answered the hermit. "I must leave now." When the Emperor insisted, the hermit said: "Many people visit my hut, and so I came here to ask you for some money." "Then", said Akbar, "why were you going away without speaking to me?" The hermit replied: "I found that you too were a beggar; you too prayed to God for money and riches.

Thereupon I said to myself: 'Why should I beg of a beggar? If I must beg, let me beg of God." (90)

'NO BEGGAR, I, FOR COMMON FRUIT'

JUST imagine Hanuman's state of mind. He didn't care for money, honour, creature comforts, or anything else. He longed only for God. When he was running away with the heavenly weapon that had been secreted in the crystal pillar, Mondodari began to tempt him with various fruits so that he might come down and drop the weapon[1]. But he couldn't be tricked so easily. In reply to her persuasions he sang this song:

Am I in need of fruit?
I have the fruit that makes this life
Fruitful indeed. Within my heart
The tree of Rama grows,
Bearing salvation for its fruits.
Under the wish-fulfilling Tree
Of Rama do I sit at ease,
Plucking whatever fruit I will
But if you speak of fruit—
No beggar, I, for common fruit.
Behold, I go
Leaving a bitter fruit for you. (91)

---

1. The story referred to here is told in the Ramayana. Ravana had received a boon as a result of which he could be killed only by a particular celestial weapon. The weapon was concealed in a crystal pillar in his palace. One day Hanuman, in the guise of an ordinary monkey, came to the palace and broke the pillar. As he was running away with weapon, he was tempted with fruits by Mandodari, Ravana's wife, so that he might give back the weapon. He soon assumed his own form and sang the song given in the text.

THORNS, DENIED, PRICK NO LESS KEENLY

ONCE, finding it difficult to reconcile the contradictory doctrines of man's free will and god's grace, two disciples of the Master went to him for a solution of the same. The Master said, "Why do you talk of free will? Everything is dependent upon the Lord's will. Our will is tied to the Lord's, like the cow to its tether. No doubt we have a cetain amount of freedom even as the cow has, within a prescribed circle. So man thinks that his will is free. But know that his will is dependent on the Lord's".

Disciples: "Is there then no necessity of practising penance, meditation and the rest? For one can as well sit quiet and say, "It is all God's will; whatever is done, is done at His will."

Sri Ramakrishna: Oh! to what effect, if you simply say that in so many words? Any amount of your verbal denial of thorns can never save you from their painful prick when you place your hand on them. Had it been entirely with man to do spiritual practices according to his will, everybody would have done so. But no; everyone can't do it, and why? But there is one thing. If you don't utilise properly the amount of strength He has given you, He never gives more. That is why self-exertion is necessary. And so everyone has to struggle hard even to become fit for the grace of God. By such endeavour, and through His grace, the sufferings of many lives can be worked out in one life. But some self-effort is absolutely necessary. Let me tell you a story:

Once Vishnu, the Lord of Goloka, cursed Narada, saying that he would be thrown into hell. At this Narada was greatly disturbed in mind; and he prayed to the Lord, singing songs of devotion, and begging Him to show where hell is and how one can go there. Vishnu then drew the map of the universe on the ground with a piece of chalk, representing the exact position of heaven and hell. Then Narada said, pointing to the part marked 'hell', "Is it like this? This is hell then!" So saying he rolled himself on the spot and exclaimed he had undergone all the sufferings of hell. Vishnu smilingly asked, "How is that?" and Narada replied: "Why, Lord, are not heaven and hell Thy creation? When Thou didst draw the map of the universe Thyself and point out to me the hell in the plan, then that place became a real hell; and as I rolled myself there, my sufferings were intense. So I do say that I have undergone the punishments of hell." Narada said all this sincerely and so Vishnu was satisfied with the explanation. (92)

SINGLE-MINDEDNESS IS ANOTHER NAME FOR DEVOTION

A MAN was angling in a lake all by himself. After a long while the float began to move. Now and then its tip touched the water. The angler was holding the rod tight in his hands, ready to pull it up, when a passer-by stopped and said, "Sir, can you tell me where Mr. Bannerji lives?' There was no reply from the angler, who was just on the point of pulling up the rod. Again and again the stranger said to him in a loud voice, "Sir can you tell me where Mr. Banerjee lives?' But the angler was unconscious of everything around him. His hands were trembling, his eyes were on the float. The stranger was annoyed and went on. When he had gone quite a way, the angler's float sank under water and with one pull of the rod he landed the fish. He wiped the sweat from his face with his towel and shouted after the stranger. "Hey!" he said, "Come here! Listen!" But the man would not turn his face. After much shouting, however, he came back and said to the angler, "Why are you shouting at me?" "What did you ask me about?" said the angler. The stranger said, "I repeated the question so many times, and now you are asking me to repeat it once more!" The angler replied, "At that time my float was about to sink; so I didn't hear a word of what you said."

A man can achieve such single-mindedness in meditation that he will see nothing, hear nothing. He will not be conscious even of touch. A snake may crawl over his body, but he will not know it. Neither of them will be aware of the other. (93)

Yearning

TO HAVE GENUINE YEARNING
FOR GOD IS TO ATTAIN HIM

A man had a daughter who became a widow when she was very young. She had never known her husband. She noticed the husbands of other girls and said one day to her father, "Where is my husband?" The father replied: "Govinda[1] is your husband. He will come to you if you call Him." At these words the girl went to her room, closed the door, and cried, to Govinda, saying: "O Govinda, come to me! Show Yourself to me! Why don't you come?" God could not resist the girl's piteous cry and appeared before her. (94)

THAT DIVINE YEARNING

GOD cannot be seen without yearning of heart, and this yearning is impossible unless one has finished with the experiences of life. Those

1. A name of Krishna.

who live surrounded by 'woman and gold', and have not yet come to the end of their experiences, do not yearn for God.

When I lived at Kamarpukur, Hriday's son, a child of four or five years old, used to spend the whole day with me. He played with toys and almost forgot everything else. But no sooner did evening come than he would say, "I want to go to my mother." I would try to cajole him in various ways and would say, "Here, I'll give you a pigeon." But he wouldn't be consoled with such things; he would weep and cry, "I want to go to my mother." He didn't enjoy playing any more. I myself wept to see his state.

One should cry for God that way, like a child. That is what it means to be restless for God. One doesn't enjoy play or food any longer. After one's experiences of the world are over, one feels restlessness and weeps for God. (95)

IF YOU ARE EARNEST

A MAN may not know the right path, but if he has bhakti and the desire to know God, then he attains Him through the force of sheer bhakti.

Once a sincere devotee set out on a pilgrimage to the temple of Jagannath in Puri. He did not know the way; he went west instead of south. He, no doubt, strayed from the right path, but always eagerly asked people the way, and they gave him the right directions, saying, 'This is not the path; follow that one.' At last the devotee was able to get to Puri and worship the Deity.

So you see, even if you are ignorant, some one will tell you the way if you are earnest. (96)

HOW A GURU TAUGHT HIS DISCIPLE TO SEE GOD

A DISCIPLE asked his teacher, "Sir, please tell me how I can see God." "Come with me," said the Guru, "and I shall show you." He took the disciple to a lake, and both of them got into the water. Suddenly the teacher pressed the disciple's head under the water. After a few moments he released him and the disciple raised his head and stood up. The Guru asked him, "How did you feel?" The disciple said, "Oh! I thought I should die; I was panting for breath." The teacher said, "When you feel like that for God, then you will know you haven't long to wait for His vision." (97)

Self-help & Self-surrender

SELF-HELP AND SELF-SURRENDER

A father was once passing through a field with his two little sons. He was carrying one of them in his arms while the other was walking along with him holding his hand. They saw a kite flying and the latter boy giving up his hold on his father's hand, began to clap his hands with joy, crying, "Behold, papa, there is a kite!" But immediately he stumbled down and got hurt. The boy who was carried by the father also clapped the hands with joy, but did not fall, as his father was holding him. The first boy represents self-help in spiritual matters, and the second self-surrender. (98)

LORD NARAYANA AND HIS SELF-DEFENDING DEVOTEE

ONCE Lakshmi and Narayana were seated in Vaikunta, when Narayana suddenly stood up. Lakshmi had been stroking his feet.

She said, "Lord, where are you going?" Narayana answered: "One of My devotees is in great danger. I must save him." With these words He went out. But He came back immediately. Lakshmi said, "Lord, why have You returned so soon?" Narayana smiled and said: "The devotee was going along the road overwhelmed with love for Me. Some washermen were drying clothes on the grass and the devotee walked over the clothes. At this the washer-men chased him and were going to beat him with their sticks. So I ran out to protect him." "But why have You come back?" asked Lakshmi. Narayana laughed and said, "I saw the devotee himself picking up a brick to throw at them. So I came back." (99)

SELF-SURRENDER KNOWS NO COMPLAINT

WHEN Rama and Lakshmana went to take their bath in Pampa Lake, they thrust their bows into the ground. Coming out of the water, Lakshmana took out his bow and found its tip stained with blood. Rama said to him: "Look, brother! Look. Perhaps we have hurt some creature." Lakshmana dug in the earth and found a big bull frog. It was dying. Rama said to the frog in a sorrowful voice: "Why didn't you croak? We should have tried to save you. You croak lustily enough when you are in the jaws of a snake." The frog said: "O Lord, when I am attacked by a snake I croak, saying: 'O Rama, save me!' This time I found that it was Rama Himself who was killing me; so I kept still." (100)

Humility:

IT'S NOT EASY TO ATTAIN TRUE HUMILITY

A man went to a sadhu and said with a great show of humility: "Sir, I am a very low person. Tell me, O Master, how I am to be saved." The sadhu, reading the heart of the man, told him, "Well, go and bring me that which is meaner than yourself." The man went out and looked all round but found nothing whatsoever meaner than himself. At last he saw his own excrement and said, "Well, here is something which is certainly worse than myself." He stretched forth his hand to take it up and carry it to the sadhu when suddenly he heard a voice say from within the ordure: "Touch me not, O sinner. I was a sweet and delicious cake, fit to be offered to the gods and in appearance so pleasing to all the spectators. But my ill-fortune brought me to you, and by your evil contact I have been reduced to such a detestable condition that men run away from me with faces turned and with handkerchiefs covering their noses. Once only did I come in contact with you and this has been my fate. What deeper degradation may I not be thrown into if you touch me again?"

The man was thus taught true humility and became the humblest of the humble. As a result he attained the highest perfection.

(101)

Tyaga and Vairagya

(RENUNCIATION AND DISPASSION)

THE HOMA BIRD

The Vedas speak of the Homa bird. It lives very high in the sky. There the mother bird lays her egg. She lives so high that the egg falls for many days. While falling it is hatched. The chick continues to fall. That also goes on for many days. In the meantime the chick develops eyes. Coming near the earth, it becomes conscious of the world. It realises it will meet certain death if it hits the ground. Then it gives a shrill cry and shoots up towards its mother. The earth means death, and it frightens the young bird; it then seeks its mother. She dwells high up in the sky, and the young bird shoots straight up in the direction. It doesn't look anywhere else.

Persons who are born with God-consciousness realise the danger of coming in contact with the world. From their very childhood they are afraid of the world, and their one thought is how to reach the mother, how to realise God. (102)

HE WENT AWAY, TOWEL ON HIS SHOULDER

A MAN was going to bathe. He had his towel on his shoulder. His wife said to him, "You are worthless. You are getting old and still you cannot give up some of your habits. You cannot live a single day without me. But look at that man! What a renouncer he is!"

Husband: "Why? What has he done?"

Wife: "He has sixteen wives and he is renouncing them one by one. You will never be able to renounce."

Husband: "Renouncing his wives one by one! You are crazy. He won't be able to renounce. If a man wants to renounce, does he do it little by little?"

Wife(smiling): "Still he is better than you."

Husband: "You are silly; you don't understand. He cannot renounce. But I can. See! Here I go!"

That is called intense renunciation. No sooner did the man discriminate than he renounced. He went away with the towel on his shoulder. He didn't turn back to settle his worldly affairs. He didn't even look back at his home.

He who wants to renounce needs great strength of mind. He must have a dare-devil attitude like a dacoit's. Before looting a house, the dacoits shout: "Kill! Murder! Loot!" (103)

DISPASSION COMES LIKE A FLOOD AND NEVER BY DROPS

How does a man come to have vairagya (dispassion)?

A wife once said to her husband: "Dear, I am very anxious about my brother. For the past one week he has been thinking of becoming an ascetic, and has been busy preparing for that life. He is trying to reduce gradually all his desires and wants." The husband replied: "Dear, be not anxious about your brother. He will never become a sannyasin. No one can become a sannyasin in that way."

"How does one become a sannyasin then?" asked the wife. "Thus" exclaimed the husband; so saying, he tore his flowing dress to pieces, took a piece and tied it round his loin, and told his wife that she and all of her sex were henceforth mothers to him. He left the house, nevermore to return. (104)

NOT UNTIL THE ILLUSION BREAKS

A GURU said to his disciple: "The world is illusory. Come away with me." "But revered sir," said the disciple, "my people at home—my father, my mother, my wife—love me so much. How can I give them up?" The guru said: "No doubt you now have this feeling of 'I' and `mine' and say that they love you; but this is all an illusion of your mind. I shall teach you a trick, and you will know whether they love you truly or not." Saying this, the teacher gave the disciple a pill and said to him: "Swallow this at home. You will appear to be a corpse, but you will not lose consciousness. You will see everything and hear everything. Then I shall come to your house and gradually you will regain your normal state."

The disciple followed the teacher's instructions and lay on his bed like a dead person. The house was filled with loud wailing. His mother, his wife, and the others lay on the ground weeping bitterly. Just then a brahmana entered the house and said to them, "What is the matter with you?" "This boy is dead", they replied. The brahmana felt the pulse and said: "How is that? No, he is not dead. I have a medicine that will cure him completely." The joy of the relatives was unbounded; it seemed to them that heaven itself had come down into their house. "But", said the brahmana, "I must tell you something else. Another person must take some of this medicine first, and then the boy must swallow the rest. But the other person will die. I see he has so many dear relatives here; one of them will certainly agree to take the medicine. I see his wife and mother crying bitterly. Surely they will not hesitate to take it".

At once the weeping stopped and all sat quiet. The mother said: "Well, this is a big family. Suppose I die; then who will look after the family?" She fell into a reflective mood. The wife, who had been crying a minute before and bemoaning her ill luck, said: "Well, he has gone the way of mortals. I have these two or three young children. Who will look after them if I die?"

The disciple saw everything and heard everything. He stood up at once and said to the teacher: "Let us go, revered sir. I will follow you." (105)

NONE WILL FOLLOW THEE AFTER DEATH

A DISCIPLE said to his Guru that his wife loved him very much and so he could not renounce the world. The disciple used to practise Hatha Yoga. To convince him of the hollowness of his plea, the Guru taught him some secrets of this branch of Yoga. One day, all of a sudden, there was great consternation in the disciple's house and wailings and sobbings were heard all around. The neighbours came running to the house, and saw the disciple in a room, quite motionless, in a peculiar convoluted posture. They all thought that life was extinct in the body. The wife of the disciple was crying: "Alas! where have you gone, dear? Why have you forsaken us? Ah! we never knew that such a calamity would befall us!" In the meantime the relatives brought a cot to take the corpse out for cremation. Then they found themselves face to face with a very serious difficulty. As the man was in a contorted posture, his body would not come out through the door. Seeing that, one of his neighbours brought an axe and began to cut the wooden frame of the door. Till then the wife was weeping in an uncontrollable fit of sorrow; but no sooner did she hear the sound of the axe than she ran to the spot, and, though still weeping, anxiously enquired what they were about. One of the neighbours told her that they were cutting the door as her husband's body could not otherwise be taken out owing to its peculiar posture. "No, no," cried out the wife, "don't do so now. I have been widowed and there is none to look after me. I have to bring up my fatherless children. If you now cut the door, it cannot be repaired again. Whatever was to happen has happened to my husband. You had better cut his hands and legs and take him out." Hearing this the Hatha Yogi at once stood up; the effect of the drug having gone by this time, and bawled out, "Woman, you want to cut my hands and legs?" And so saying, he went away with his Guru renouncing hearth and home. (106)

TODAY'S IMITATION IS TOMORROW'S INSPIRATION

A THIEF entered the palace of a king in the dead of night and overheard the king saying to the queen, "I shall give my daughter in marriage to one of those sadhus (holy men) who are dwelling on the bank of the river." The thief thought within himself: "Well, here is good luck for me. I will go and sit among the sadhus tomorrow in the disguise of a sadhu, and perchance I may succeed in getting the king's daughter." The next day he did so. When the king's officers came soliciting the sadhus to marry the king's daughter, none of them consented to it. At last they came to the thief in the guise of a sadhu, and made the same proposal to him. The thief kept quiet. The officers went back and told the king that there was a young sadhu who might be influenced to marry the princess, and that there was no other who would consent. The king then came to the sadhu in person and earnestly entreated him to honour him by accepting the hand of his daughter. But the heart of the thief was changed at the king's visit. He thought within himself: "I have only assumed the garb of a sadhu, and behold! the king comes to me and is all entreaties. Who can say what better things may not be in store for me if I become a real sadhu!" These thoughts so strongly affected him that, instead of marrying under false pretences, he began to mend his ways from that very day and exerted himself to become a true sadhu. He did not marry at all, and ultimately became one of the most pious ascetics of his day. The counterfeiting of a good thing sometimes leads to unexpected good results. (107)

SIMULATION OF HOLINESS MAY BECOME A STIMULATION FOR IT

ONE night a fisherman went into a garden and cast his net into the lake in order to steal some fish. The owner heard him and surrounded him with his servants. They brought lighted torches and began to search for him. In the mean time the fisherman smeared his body with ashes and sat under a tree, pretending to be a holy man. The owner and his men searched a great deal but could not find the thief. All they saw was a holy man covered with ashes, meditating under a tree. The next day the news spread in the neighbourhood that a great sage was staying in the garden. People gathered there and saluted him with offerings of fruits, flowers, and sweets. Many also offered silver and copper coins. "How strange!" thought the fisherman, "I am not a genuine holy man, and still people show such devotion to me. I shall certainly realize God if I become a true sadhu. There is no doubt about it." (108)

EQUAL VISION IS THE FIRST AND LAST SIGN OF RENUNCIATION

A HUSBAND and wife renounced the world and together undertook a pilgrimage to various holy shrines. Once as they were walking along a road, the husband, being a little ahead of the wife, saw a piece of diamond on the road. Immediately he began to scratch the ground to hide the diamond in it, thinking that if his wife saw it perchance she might be moved to avarice, and thus lose the merit of renunciation. While he was thus scratching the ground, the wife came up and asked him what he was doing. He gave her, in an apologetic tone, an evasive reply. She, however, finding out the diamond and reading his thoughts remarked, "Why did you leave the world if you still feel the distinction between the diamond and dust?" (109)

HARD ARE THE RULES FOR A SANNYASI

THE rules for a sannyasi are extremely hard. He cannot have the slightest contact with 'woman and gold.' He must not accept money with his own hands and he must not even allow it to be left near him.

Lakshminarayan Marwari, a Vedantist, used to come here[1] very often. One day he saw a dirty sheet on my bed and said: "I shall invest ten thousand rupees in your name. The interest will enable you to pay your expenses." The moment he uttered these words, I fell unconscious, as if struck by a stick. Regaining consciousness I said to him: "If you utter such words again, you had better not come here. It is impossible for me to touch money. It is also impossible for me to keep it near me." He was a very clever fellow. He said:

"Then you too have the idea of acceptance and rejection. In that case you haven't attained Perfect Knowledge." "My dear sir," I said, "I haven't gone that far." Lakshminarayanan then wanted to leave the money with Hriday. I said to him: "That will not do. If you leave it with Hriday, then I shall

1. At the Dakshineswar Temple Garden to visit Sri Ramakrishna.

instruct him to spend it as I wish. If he does not comply, I shall be angry. The very contact of money is bad. No, you can't leave it with Hriday. Won't an object kept near a mirror be reflected in it?" (110)

A BAHURUPI IMPERSONATING SIVA

A *Bahurupi*[1] disguised himself as Siva and visited a house. The master of the house wanted to give him a rupee, but he did not accept it. Then the mendicant went home, removed his disguise, came back to the gentleman, and asked for the rupee. "Why didn't you accept it before?" he was asked. He said: "I was impersonating Siva, a sannayasi. I couldn't touch money at that time." (111)

HOLD HARD YOUR SPADE

AT one time there was a drought in a certain part of the country. The farmers began to cut long channels to bring water to their fields. One farmer was stubbornly determined. He took a vow that he would not stop digging

1. A professional impersonator.

until the channel connected his field with the river. He set to work. The time came for his bath, and his wife sent their daughter to him with oil. "Father," said the girl, "it is already late. Rub your body with oil and take your bath." "Go away," thundered the farmer. "I have too much to do now." It was past midday and the farmer was still at work in his field. He didn't even think of his bath. Then his wife came and said: "Why haven't you taken your bath? The food is getting cold. You overdo everything. You can finish the rest tomorrow or even today after dinner." The farmer scolded her furiously and ran at her, spade in hand, crying: "What! Have you no sense? There's no rain. The crops are dying. What will the children eat? You'll starve to death. I have taken a vow not to think of bath and food today before I bring water to my field." The wife saw his state of mind and ran away in fear. Through a whole day's back-breaking labour the farmer managed by evening to connect his field with the river. Then he sat down and watched the water flowing into his field with a murmuring sound. His mind was filled with peace and joy. He went home, called his wife and said to her, "Now give me some oil and prepare a smoke." With serene mind he finished his bath and meal, and retired to bed, where he snored to his heart's content. The determination he showed is an example of strong renunciation.

Now, there was another farmer who was also digging a channel to bring water to his field. His wife, too, came to the field and said to him, "It's very late. Come home. It is not necessary to overdo things." The farmer did not protest much, but put aside his spade and said to his wife, "Well I will go home since you ask me to." That man could never succeed in irrigating his field. This is the case of mild renunciation. (112)

AS YOU GO FROM NEAR TO NEARER

A MUSSALMAN, while saying his prayers, shouted: "O Allah! O Allah!" Another person said to him: "You are calling on Allah. That's all right. But why are you shouting like that? Don't you know that He hears the sound of the anklets on the feet of an ant?"

When the mind is united with God, one sees him very near, in one's own heart. But you must remember one thing. The more you realize this unity, the farther your mind is withdrawn from worldly things. There is the story of Vilwamangal in the *Bhaktamala*. He used to visit a prostitute. One night he was very late in going to her house. He had been detained at home by the *Sraddha* ceremony of his father and mother. In his hands he was carrying the food offered in the ceremony, to feed his mistress. His whole soul was so set upon the woman that he was not at all conscious of his movements. He did not even know how he was walking. There was a Yogi seated on the path, meditating on God with his eyes closed. Vilwamangal stepped on him. The yogi became angry, and cried out: "What? Are you blind? I have been thinking of God and you step on my body!" "I beg your pardon," said Vilwamangal, "but may I ask you something? I have been unconscious, thinking of a prostitute, and you are conscious of the outer world though thinking of God. What kind of meditation is that?" In the end Vilwamangal renounced the world and went away in order to worship God. He said to the prostitute: 'You are my Guru. You have taught me how one should yearn for God." He addressed the prostitute as his mother and gave her up. (113)

THE KING AND THE PANDIT

THERE was a king who used daily to hear the *Bhagavata* recited by a pandit. Every day, after explaining the sacred book, the pandit would say to the king, "O King, have you understood what I have said?" And everyday the king would reply, "You had better understand it first yourself." The pandit would return home and think: "Why does the king talk to me that way day after day? I explain the texts to him so clearly, and he says to me, 'You had better understand it first yourself.' What does he mean?" The pandit used to practise spiritual discipline. A few days later he came to realise that God alone is real and everything else—house, family, wealth, friends, name, and fame—illusory. Convinced of the unreality of the world, he renounced it. As he left home he asked a man to take this message to the king: "O king, I now understand." (114)

EVEN IF YOU WISH TO RENOUNCE THE WORLD

MAN cannot renounce the world even if he wishes, because he is thwarted by the karmas that are bearing fruit in the present birth and by the impressions of previous actions left on the mind (*Prarabdha* and *Samskara*).

Once a Yogi asked a king to sit down near him and meditate upon God. To him the King replied, "No, Sir, that cannot be. I can remain near you, but still the thirst for worldly enjoyment will be with me. If I remain in this forest, perhaps there will arise a kingdom within it, as I am still destined to enjoy." (115)

WHEN RENUNCIATION BECOMES THE LIFE-BREATH

No Spiritual progress is possible without the renunciation of 'woman and gold'. I renounced these three: land, wife and wealth. Once I went to the Registry office to register some land, the title of which was in the name of Raghuvir.[1] The officer asked me to sign my name; but I did not do it because I couldn't feel that it was 'my' land. I was shown much respect as the guru of Keshab Sen. They presented me with mangoes. But I couldn't carry them home. A Sannyasi cannot lay things up.

How can one expect to attain God without renunciation? Suppose one thing is placed upon another; how can you get the second without removing the first? (116)

A GHOST SOUGHT A COMPANION

A GHOST sought a companion. It is said that a man who dies on a Saturday or Tuesday becomes a ghost. Therefore, whenever the

---

1. The tutelary Deity at the ancestral home of Sri Ramakrishna.

ghost saw anybody fall from a roof or stumble and faint on the road on either side of those days, he would run to him, hoping that the man, through an accidental death, would become a ghost and be his companion. But such was his ill luck that everyone revived. The poor thing could not get a companion.

It is very difficult to find a person who has totally renounced the world. (117)

Book the Third

Brahman

A SALT DOLL WENT TO FATHOM THE OCEAN

Once a salt doll went to measure the depth of the ocean. It wanted to tell others how deep the water was. But this it could never do, for no sooner did it get into the water than it melted. Now, who was there to report the ocean's depth?

What Brahman is cannot be described. In samadhi one attains the knowledge of Brahman—one realises Brahman. In that state reasoning stops altogether, and man becomes mute. He has no power to describe the nature of Brahman. (118)

FOUR FRIENDS LOOKED BEYOND

ONCE four friends, in the course of a walk, saw a place enclosed by a wall. The wall was very high. They all became eager to know what was inside. One of them climbed to the top of the wall. What he saw on looking inside made him speechless with wonder. He only cried, 'Ah! Ah!' and dropped in. He could not give any information about what he saw. The others too climbed the wall, uttered the same cry, 'Ah! Ah!' and jumped in. Now who could tell what was inside!

What Brahman is cannot be described. Even he who knows it cannot talk about it. (119)

WHERE SILENCE IS ELOQUENT AND SPEECH DOTH FALTER

A MAN had two sons. The father sent them to a preceptor to learn the knowledge of Brahman. After a few years they returned from their preceptor's house and bowed low before their father. Wanting to measure the depth of their knowledge of Brahman, he first questioned the older of the two boys. "My child," he said, "You have studied all the scriptures. Now, tell me, what is the nature of Brahman?" The boy began to explain Brahman by reciting various texts from the Vedas. The father did not say anything. Then he asked the younger son the same question. But the boy remained silent and stood with eyes cast down. No word escaped his lips. The father was pleased and said to him: "My child, you have understood a little of Brahman. What It is cannot be expressed in words." (120)

NEITHER 'YES' NOR 'NO!'

THE husband of a young girl has come to his father-in-law's house and is seated in the drawing-room with other young men of his age. The girl and her friends are looking at them through the window. Her friends do not know her husband and ask her, pointing to one young man, "Is that your husband?" "No," she answers, smiling. They point to another young man and ask if he is her husband. Again she answers, "No." They repeat the question, referring to a third, and she gives the same answer. At last they point to her husband and ask, "Is he the one?" She says neither yes nor no, but only smiles and keeps quiet. Her friends realize that he is her husband.

One becomes silent on realising the true nature of Brahman.

THE KING AND THE MAGICIAN

As you go nearer to God you see less and less of His *upādhis,* His attributes. A devotee at first may see the Deity as the ten-armed Divine Mother; when he goes nearer he sees her possessed of six arms; still nearer, he sees the Deity as the two-armed Gopala. The nearer he comes to the Deity, the fewer attributes he sees. At last, when he comes into the presence of the Deity, he sees only Light without any attribute.

Listen a little to the Vedantic reasoning. A magician came to a king to show his magic. When the magician moved away a little, the king saw a rider on horse-back approaching him. He was brilliantly arrayed and had various weapons in his hands. The king and the audience began to reason out what was real in the phenomenon before them. Evidently the horse was not real, nor the robes nor the armours. At last they found out beyond the shadow of a doubt that the rider alone was there. The significance of this is that Brahman alone is real and the world unreal. Nothing whatsoever remains if you analyse. (122)

WHEN FACE TO FACE

WHERE the mind attains peace by practising the discipline of 'Neti, neti,' there Brahman is.

The king dwells in the inmost room of the palace, which has seven gates. The visitor comes to the first gate. There he sees a lordly person with a large retinue, surrounded on all sides by pomp and grandeur. The visitor asks his companion, "Is he the king?" "No," says his friend with a smile.

At the second and other gates he repeats the same question to his friend. He finds that the nearer he comes to the inmost part of the palace, the greater is the glory, pomp, and grandeur.

When he passes the seventh gate he does not ask his companion whether it is the king; he stands speechless at the king's immeasurable glory. He realizes that he is face to face with the king. He hasn't the slightest doubt about it. (123)

'BEHOLD, O KING! BEHOLD'

ONCE a king asked a yogi to impart Knowledge to him in one word. The yogi said, "All right; you will get knowledge in one word." After a while a magician came to the king. The king saw the magician moving two of his fingers rapidly and heard him exclaim, "Behold, O king, Behold." The king looked at him amazed when, after a few minutes, he saw the two fingers becoming one. The magician moved that one finger rapidly and said, "Behold, O king! Behold."

The implication of the story is that Brahman and the Primal Energy at first appear to be two. But after attaining knowledge of Brahman one does not see the two. Then there is no differentiation; it is One, without a second—Advaita—non-duality. (124)

AN ANT WENT TO A SUGAR HILL

MEN often think they have understood Brahman fully.

Once an ant went to a sugar hill. One grain filled its stomach. Taking another grain in its mouth it started homeward. On its way it thought, "Next time I shall carry home the whole hill." That is the way shallow minds think. They don't know that Brahman is beyond words and thought. However great a man may be, how much can he know of Brahman? Sukadeva and sages like him may have been big ants; but even they at the utmost could carry eight or ten grains of sugar! (125)

HE EATS, YET EATS NOT

ONCE Vyasadeva was about to cross the Jamuna. The gopis also were there. They wanted to go to the other side of the river to sell curd, milk, and cream. But there was no ferry at that time. They were all worried about how to cross the river, when Vyasa said to them, "I am very hungry." The milkmaids fed him with milk and cream. He finished almost all their food. Then Vyasa said to the river, "O Jamuna, if I have not eaten anything, then your waters will part and we shall walk through." It so happened. The river parted and a pathway was formed between the waters. Following that path, the gopis and Vyasa crossed the river.

Vyasa had said, "If I have not eaten anything." That means, the real man is Pure Atman. Atman is unattached and beyond Prakriti. It has neither hunger nor thirst; It knows neither birth nor death; It does not age, nor does It die. It is immutable as Mount Sumeru. (126)

ALL PURE SPIRIT

ALL doubts disappear when one sees God. It is one thing to hear of God, but quite a different thing to see Him. A man cannot have one hundred per cent conviction through mere hearing. But if he beholds God face to face, then he is wholly convinced.

Formal worship drops away after the vision of God. It was thus that my worship in the temple came to an end. I used to worship the deity in the Kali Temple. It was suddenly revealed to me that everything is Pure Spirit. The utensils of worship, the altar, the door-frame—all Pure Spirit. Then like a mad man I began to shower flowers in all directions. Whatever I saw I worshipped. (127)

Aspects of the Divine

THE CHAMELEON

Once a man entered a wood and saw a small animal on a tree. He came back and told another man that he had seen a creature of a beautiful red colour on a certain tree. The second man replied: "When I went into the wood, I also saw that animal. But why do you call it red? It is green." Another man who was present contradicted them both and insisted that it was yellow. Presently others arrived and contended that it was grey, violet, blue, and so forth and so on. At last they started quarrelling among themselves. To settle the dispute they all went to the tree. They saw a man sitting under it. On being asked, he replied: "Yes, I live under this tree and I know the animal very well. All your descriptions are true. Sometimes it appears red, sometimes yellow, and at other times blue, violet, grey and so forth. It is a chameleon. And sometimes it has no colour at all. Now it has a colour, and now it has none."

In like manner, one who constantly thinks of God can know His real nature; he alone knows that God reveals Himself to seekers in various forms and aspects. God has attributes; then again He has none. Only the man who lives under the tree knows that the chameleon can appear in various colours, and he knows further that the animal at times has no colour at all. It is the others who suffer from the agony of futile argument. (128)

MAN WITH A TUB OF DYE

NATURALLY the doubt arises in the mind: if God is formless, how then can He have form? Further, if He has a form, why does He have so many forms?

These things do not become clear until one has realized God. He assumes different forms and reveals Himself in different ways for the sake of His devotees.

A man kept a solution of dye in a tub. Many people came to him to have their clothes dyed. He would ask a customer, "What colour should you like to have your cloth dyed?" If the customer wanted red, then the man would dip the cloth in the tub and say, "Here is your cloth dyed red." If another customer wanted his cloth dyed yellow, the man would dip his cloth in the same tub and say, "Here is your cloth dyed yellow." If a customer wanted his cloth dyed blue, the man would dip it in the same tub and say, "Here is your cloth dyed blue." Thus he would dye the clothes of his customers different colours, dipping them all in the same solution. One of the customers watched all this with amazement. The man asked him, "Well! What colour do you want for your cloth?" The customer said, "Brother, dye my cloth the colour of the dye in your tub." (129)

WHAT THE DIVINE MOTHER REVEALED TO ME

Do you know where those who speak of the formless God make their mistake? It is where they say that God is formless only, and that those who differ from them are wrong.

But I know God is both with and without form. And he may have many more aspects. It is possible for Him to be everything.

The Chitsakti, Mahamaya, has become the twenty-four cosmic principles. One day as I was meditating, my mind wandered away to Rashke's house. He is a scavenger. I said to my mind, 'Stay there, you rogue!' The Divine Mother revealed to me that the men and women in this house were mere masks; inside them was the same Divine Power, Kundalini, that rises up through the six spiritual centres of the body. (130)

HOW A MONK KNEW THE TRUTH ABOUT GOD

A CERTAIN monk went to the temple of Jagannath at Puri. He had doubts as to whether God is with form or without form. When he saw the holy image, he desired to examine it and settle his doubt. He passed his staff from the left to the right in order to feel if it touched the image. For a time he could not see anything or feel anything with the staff. So he decided that God was without form. When he was about to pass the staff from the right to the left, it touched the image. So the monk decided that God is both with form and without form. (131)

GOD ALONE HAS BECOME ALL THINGS

AT one time Rama was overpowered by the spirit of renunciation. Dasaratha, worried at this, went to the sage Vasishtha and begged him to persuade Rama not to give up the world. The sage came to Rama and found him in a gloomy mood. The fire of intense renunciation had been raging in the Prince's mind. Vasishtha said: "Rama, why should you renounce the world? Is the world outside God? Reason with me." Rama realized that the world had evolved from the supreme Brahman. So he said nothing. (132)

STRIP NAME AND FORM AND LOOK BEYOND

ONCE a sadhu placed his disciple in a magnificent garden with the intention of imparting to him the knowledge of the real Self and went away. After a few days he came back and asked the disciple, "Do you feel any want, my boy?" On being answered in the affirmative, he left with him a fair woman named Shyama, and advised him to take fish and meat freely. After a considerable time he came again and asked the same question as before. This time the disciple replied, "No, I have no want, thank you". The sadhu then called both the disciple and Shyama to him and pointing to Shyama's hands, asked the disciple, "Can you tell me what these are?" "Why, these are Shyama's hands", replied the disciple. He put the same question several times, pointing to Shyama's eyes, nose, and other parts of the body, and the disciple gave appropriate answers. Presently the idea struck the disciple, "I am talking of everything as Shyama's 'this' and Shyama's 'that'. What then is this Shyama?" Bewildered, he asked his Guru the question, "But who is this Shyama to whom belong these eyes, ears and the rest?" The sadhu said, "If you wish to know who this Shyama is, come with me, and I will enlighten you". So saying, he revealed to him the secret. (133)

FEW, VERY FEW ARE THEY

A RICH man said to his servant: "Take this diamond to the market and let me know how different people price it. Take it, first of all, to the egg-plant seller." The servant took the diamond to the egg-plant seller. He examined it, turning it over in the palm of his hand, and said, "Brother, I can give nine seers of egg-plants for it." "Friend," said the servant, "a little more, say, ten seers." The egg-plant seller replied: "No, I have already quoted above the market price. You may give it to me if that price suits you." The servant laughed. He went back to his master and said: "Sir, he would give me only nine seers of egg-plants and not one more. He said he had offered more than the market price." The master smiled and said: "Now take it to the cloth dealer. The other man deals only in egg-plants. What does he know about a diamond? The cloth-dealer has a little more capital. Let us see how much he offers for it." The servant went to the cloth-dealer and said: "Will you buy this? How much will you pay for it?" The merchant said: "Yes, it is a good thing. I can make a nice ornament out of it. I will give you nine hundred rupees for it." "Brother," said the servant, "offer a little more and I will sell it to you. Give me at least a thousand rupees." The cloth-dealer said: "Friend, don't press me for more. I have offered more than the market price. I cannot give a rupee more. Suit yourself." Laughing, the servant returned to his master and said: "He won't give a rupee more than nine hundred. He too said he had quoted above the market price." The master said with a laugh: "Now take it to a jeweller. Let us see what he has to say." The servant went to the jeweller. The jeweller glanced at the diamond and said at once, "I will give you one hundred thousand rupees for it."

One offers a price for an article according to one's capital. Can all comprehend the Indivisible Satchidananda? Only twelve rishis could recognize Ramachandra. All cannot recognise an Incarnation of God. Some take him for an ordinary man, some for a holy person, and only a few recognise him as an Incarnation. (134)

SHE CAME AND WENT AWAY

BY the roadside on the way to Kamarpukur is Ranjit Raya's lake. Bhagavati, the Divine Mother, was born as his daughter. Even now people hold an annual festival there in the month of Chaitra, in honour of this divine daughter.

Ranjit Roy was the landlord of that part of the country. Through the power of his *tapasya* he obtained the Divine Mother as his daughter. He was very fond of her, and she too was much attached to him; she hardly left his presence. One day Ranjit Roy was engaged in the duties of his estate. He was very busy. The girl, with her childlike nature, was constantly interrupting him, saying: "Father, what is this? What is that?" Ranjit Roy tried, with sweet words, to persuade her not to disturb him, and said: "My child, please leave me alone. I have much work to do." But the girl would not go away. At last absent-mindedly, the father said, "Get out of here!" On this pretext she left home. A pedlar of conch-shell articles was going along the road. From him she took a pair of bracelets for her wrists. When he asked for the price, she said that he could get the money from a certain box in her home. Then she disappeared. Nobody saw her again. In the meantime the pedlar came to the house and asked for the price of his bracelets. When she was not to be found at home, her relatives began to run about looking for her. Ranjit Roy sent people in all directions to search for her. The money owed to the pedlar was found in the box, as she had indicated. Ranjit Roy was weeping bitterly, when people came running to him and said that they had noticed something in the lake. They all ran there and saw an arm, with conch-shell bracelets on the wrist, being waved above the water. A moment afterwards it disappeared. Even now people worship her as the Divine Mother at the time of the annual festival.

By dint of austerity, a man may obtain God as his son. God reveals Himself in many ways; sometimes as man, sometimes in other divine forms made of spirit. (135)

THUS SAW ARJUNA

ACCORDING to the Jnani there is no Incarnation of God.

Krishna said to Arjuna, "You speak of Me as an Incarnation of God. Let Me show you something. Come with Me." Arjuna had followed Sri Krishna a short distance, when Sri Krishna asked him, "What do you see there?" Arjuna replied, "A big tree with black berries hanging in bunches." Krishna said, "Those are not black berries. Go nearer and look at them." Arjuna went nearer and saw that they were Krishnas hanging in bunches. "Do you see now", said Krishna "how many Krishnas like Me have grown there?" (136)

NOTHING IS IMPOSSIBLE FOR HIM

ONE day in course of a conversation about God, Mathur Babu observed, "God too must abide by his own laws. He has no power to transcend them." "What an absurd proposition!", I exclaimed. "One who has made a law can repeal it at pleasure or make a new law in its place." "How can that be?" said Mathur. "A plant that produces only red flowers cannot produce flowers of any other colour,—white, for instance, for such is the law. I should like to see God produce white flowers from a plant bearing only red flowers." "That too He can do," answered I, "for everything depends on His will." Mathur was not convinced. The next day, while taking a stroll in the temple garden I came across a chine-rose plant with two flowers on the same stalk, one of which was red and the other snow-white. I broke off the branch to show it to Mathur, who felt highly surprised at the sight of it and exclaimed, "Father, I will never more argue a point with thee!" (137)

TO HIM THESE ARE MERE DUST AND STRAW

ONCE a thief broke into the temple of Vishnu and robbed the image of its jewels. Mathur Babu and I went to the temple to see what the matter was. Addressing the image, Mathur said bitterly: "What a shame, Lord! You are so worthless! The thief took all the ornaments from your body, and You couldn't do a thing about it?" Thereupon I said to Mathur: "Shame on you! How improper your words are! To God, the jewels you talk so much about are only lumps of clay. Lakshmi, the goddess of Fortune, is His consort. Do you mean to say that He should spend sleepless nights because a thief has taken your few rupees? You must not say such things." (138)

NATURE OF GOD

GOD has the nature of a child.

A child is sitting with gems in the skirt of his cloth. Many a person passes by him along the road. Many of them pray to him for gems. But he hides the gems with his hands and says turning away his face, "No, I will not give any away." But another man comes along. He does not ask for the gems, and yet the child runs after him and offers him the gems, begging him to accept them. (139)

GOD IS UNDER THE CONTROL OF HIS DEVOTEES

SOME Sikhs said to me in front of the Kali temple, "God is compassionate". I said, "To whom is he compassionate?" "Why revered sir, to all of us", said the Sikhs. I said: "We are His children. Does compassion to one's own children mean much? A father must look after his children; or do you expect the people of the neighbourhood to bring them up? Well, won't those who say that God is compassionate ever understand that we are God's children and not someone else's?"

Should we not, then, address God as compassionate? Of course we should, as long as we practise sadhana. After realizing God, one rightly feels that God is our Father or Mother. As long as we have not realized God, we feel that we are far away from Him, children of someone else.

During the stage of sadhana one should describe God by all His attributes. One day Hazra said to Narendra: "God is Infinity. Infinite is His splendour. Do you think He will accept your offerings of sweets and bananas or listen to your music? This is a mistaken notion of yours." Narendra at once sank ten fathoms. So I said to Hazra, "You villain! Where will these youngsters be if you talk to them like that?" How can a man live if he gives up devotion? No doubt God has infinite splendour; yet He is under the control of His devotees. A rich man's gate-keeper comes to the parlour where his master is seated with his friends. He stands on one side of the room. In his hand he has something covered with a cloth. He is very hesitant. The master asks him, "Well, gate-keeper, what have you in your hand?" Very hesitantly the servant takes out a custard-apple from under the cover, places it in front of his master, and says, "Sir, it is my desire that you eat this." The master is impressed by his servant's devotion. With great love he takes the fruit in his hand and says: "Ah! This is a very nice custard-apple. Where did you pick it? You must have taken a great deal of trouble to get it."

God is under the control of His devotees. King Duryodhana was very attentive to Krishna and said to Him, "Please have your meal here." But the Lord went to Vidura's hut.

He was very fond of His devotee. He ate Vidura's simple rice and greens as if they were celestial food. (140)

ALL ELSE IS UNREAL

THE truth is that God alone is real and all else is unreal. Men, universe, house, children—all these are like the magic of the magician. The magician strikes his wand and says: "Come delusion! Come confusion!" Then he says to the audience, "Open the lid of the pot; see the birds fly into the sky." But the magician alone is real and his magic unreal. The unreal exists for a second and then vanishes.

Siva was seated in Kailas. His companion Nandi was near Him. Suddenly a terrific noise arose. "Revered sir," asked Nandi, "what does that mean?" Siva said: "Ravana is born. That is the meaning!" A few moments later another terrific noise was heard. "Now what is this noise?" Nandi asked. Siva said with a smile, "Ravana is dead."

Birth and death are like magic. You see the magic for a second and then it disappers.

God alone is real and all else unreal. Water alone is real; its bubbles appear and disappear. They disappear into the very water from which they rise. (141)

THE LURE OF DIVINE LILA

AFTER the destruction of Ravana at Rama's hands, Nikasha, Ravana's mother, began to run away for fear of her life. Lakshmana said to Rama: "Revered brother, please explain this strange thing to me. This Nikasha is an old woman who has suffered a great deal from the loss of her many sons, and yet she is so afraid of losing her own life that she is taking to her heels!" Rama bade her come near, gave her assurance of safety, and asked her why she was running away. Nikasha answered, "O Rama, I am able to witness all this lila of Yours because I am still alive. I want to live longer so that I may see the many more things You will do on this earth." (142)

A PEACOCK THAT TASTED OPIUM

A MAN once fed a peacock with a pill of opium at four o'clock in the afternoon. The next day, exactly at that time, the peacock came back. It had felt the intoxication of the drug and returned just in time to have another dose.

Similarly, a devotee who had the good fortune to meet the Master felt an uncontrollable desire to meet him again and again. (143)

KA! KA! KA!

THERE was a pundit who was tremendously vain. He did not believe in the forms of God. But who can understand the inscrutable ways of the Divine? God revealed Himself to him as the Primal Power. The vision made the pundit unconscious for a long time. After regaining partial consciousness he uttered only the sound 'Ka! Ka! Ka!' He could not fully pronounce 'Kali'. (144)

INSCRUTABLE ARE THE WAYS OF GOD

HOW can we understand the ways of God through our small intellects?

As Bhishma lay dying on his bed of arrows, the Pandava brothers and Krishna stood around him. They saw tears flowing from the eyes of the great hero. Arjuna said to Krishna: "Friend, how surprising it is! Even such a man as our grandsire Bhishma—truthful, self-restrained, supremely wise, and one of the eight Vasus—weeps, through maya, at the hour of death." Sri Krishna asked Bhishma about it. Bhishma replied: "O Krishna, You know very well that this is not the cause of my grief. I am thinking that there is no end to the Pandavas' sufferings, though God Himself is their charioteer. A thought like this makes me feel that I have understood nothing of the ways of God, and so I weep." (145)

AN INTERESTING INCIDENT!

PADMALOCHANA was a man of deep wisdom. He had great respect for me, though at that time I constantly repeated the name of the Divine Mother. He was the courtpandit of the Maharaja of Burdwan. Once he came to Calcutta and went to live in a garden house near Kamarhati. I felt a desire to see him and sent Hriday there to learn if the pandit had any vanity. I was told that he had none. Then I met him. Though a man of great knowledge and scholarship, he began to weep on hearing me sing Ramprasad's devotional songs. We talked together a long while; conversation with nobody else gave me such satisfaction.

Padmalochan told me an interesting incident. Once a meeting was called to decide which of the two deities, Siva or Brahmā, was the greater, and unable to come to any decision, the pandits at last referred the matter to Padmalochan. With characteristic guilelessness he said: "How do I know? Neither I nor any of my ancestors back to the fourteenth generation have seen Siva or Brahmā!" (146)

WHY NOT THROUGH A MAN?

It is God Himself who plays about as human beings. If God can be worshipped through a clay image why not through a man?

Once a merchant was shipwrecked. He floated to the shore of Ceylon, where Vibhishana was the king of the monsters. Vibhishana ordered his servants to bring the merchant to him. At the sight of him Vibhishana was overwhelmed with joy and said: "Ah! He looks like my Rama. The same human form!" He adorned the merchant with robes and jewels, and worshipped him. When I first heard this story, I felt such joy that I cannot describe it. (147)

WHEN GOD LAUGHS

GOD laughs on two occasions. He laughs when the physician says to the patient's mother, "Don't be afraid, mother, I shall certainly cure your boy." God laughs saying to Himself, "I am going to take his life, and this man says he will save it!" The physician thinks he is the master, forgetting that God is the Master. God laughs again when two brothers divide their land with a string, saying to each other, "This side is mine, that side is yours." He laughs and says to Himself, "The universe belongs to Me, but they say they own this portion or that portion." (148)

HOW DO YOU EXPLAIN THAT?

ONE must believe in the Divine Presence in the image.

Once I went to Vishnupur.[1] The Raja of that place has several fine temples. In one of them there is an image of the Divine Mother, called Mrinmayi. There are several lakes near the temple, known as the Lalbandh, Krishnabandh, and so on. In the water of one of the lakes I could smell the ointments that women use for their hair. How do you explain that? I didn't know at that time that the woman devotees offer ointments to the Goddess Mrinmayi while visiting Her temple. Near the lake I went into samadhi, though I had not yet seen the image in the temple. In that state I saw the divine form from the waist up, rising from the water. (149)

WHO CAN TELL?

TAKE the case of a patient. Nature has almost cured him, when the physician prescribes a herb and asks him to drink its juice. After taking the medicine he is completely cured. Now, is the patient cured by the medicine; or does he get well by himself? Who can tell?

---

1. A place, on the way from Calcutta to Kamarpukur, Sri Ramakrishna's birth place.

Lakshmana said to Lava and Kusa,[1] "You are mere children, you don't know Rama's power. At the touch of His feet, Ahalya[2], who had been turned into a stone, got back her human form." Lava and Kusa said, "Revered sir, we know that! We have heard the story. The stone became Ahalya because of the power of the holy man's words. The sage Gautama said to her: 'In the Treatayuga, Rama will pass this hermitage. You will become a human being again at the touch of His feet.' "

Now, who can tell whether the miracle happened in order that the sage's words should be fulfilled or on account of Rama's holiness? (150)

---

1. Rama's two sons.
2. The beautiful and devoted wife of a great sage named Gautama. Indra, the king of heaven, infatuated with her beauty, seduced her, impersonating her husband. The sage, coming to know of this, cursed her and turned her into a stone; but he said that the touch of Rama's feet would restore her human form. Indra, too, received his share of the curse, as a result of which he had a thousand eruptions on his body. Hence he is known as the "thousand-eyed God."

Man in Divine State

"THE WINE OF HEAVENLY BLISS"

The son said to the father, "Father, you taste a little wine, and after that, if you ask me to give up drinking, I shall do so." After drinking the wine, the father said: "Son, you may give it up. I have no objection. But I am certainly not going to give it up myself!" (151)

THEY WANDER IN MANY DISGUISES

ONCE a God-intoxicated sadhu came to the Kali temple. One day he received no food, but, though feeling hungry, he did not ask for any. Seeing a dog eating the remnants of a feast thrown away in a corner, he went there and embracing the dog, said, "Brother, how is it that you eat alone, without giving me a share?" So saying he began to eat along with the dog. Having finished his meal in this strange company, the sadhu entered the temple of Mother Kali and prayed with such an ecstasy of devotion as to send a thrill throughout the temple. When, after finishing his prayer he was going to leave, I asked Hriday to watch and follow the man and to communicate to me what he might say. Hriday followed him for some distance, when the sadhu turning round, enquired, "Why do you follow me?" Hriday said, "Revered sir, give me some teaching!" The sadhu replied, "When the water of this ditch and yonder Ganges appear as one and the same in your sight, when the sound of this flageolet and the noise of that crowd have no distinction to your ear, then you will reach the state of true knowledge." So saying he hastened away.

When I heard this from Hriday I remarked, "That man has reached the true state of ecstasy, the true state of knowledge."

The Siddhas roam about sometimes like guileless children, sometimes like ghouls and at other times like mad men. Indeed, they wander in many disguises. (152)

VISHNU EVERYWHERE

THERE was a holy man who used to live in a state of ecstasy and would not speak with any one. He was regarded as a lunatic. One day having begged some food in the village, he took his seat by the side of a dog and fell to eating. A strange sight now presented itself and attracted a crowd of spectators, for the holy man would put one morsel into his own mouth and the next into that of the dog, so that the man and the beast went on eating together like a pair of friends. Some of the spectators began to laugh at the holy man as being a mad fellow. Thereupon he said,

"Why do you laugh?
Vishnu is seated with *Vishnu;*
Vishnu is feeding *Vishnu;*
Why do you laugh, O *Vishnu?*
Whatever is, is Vishnu." (153)

WHERE IS THE MISERY FOR HIM WHO SEES THE ONE?

ONCE there came to Dakshineswar two sadhus who were father and son. The son had attained true knowledge, but the father had not. Both were sitting in the room where Sri Ramakrishna lived and were talking with him. In the meantime, a young cobra came out of a rat-hole and bit the son. Seeing that, the father was terribly frightened and began to call all the people around. But the son sat quiet, and that puzzled the father still more. When he asked the son why he was sitting quiet, the son laughed and was heard to explain: "Which is the snake and whom has it bitten?" He had realised the Unity, and hence he could not make any distinction between a man and a snake. (154)

BOTH FRIEND AND FOE THE SAINTS ADORE

THERE was a monastery in a certain place. The monks residing there went out daily to beg their food. One day a monk, while out for his alms, saw a landlord beating a man mercilessly. The compassionate monk stepped in and asked the landlord to stop. But the landlord was filled with anger and turned his wrath against the innocent monk. He beat the monk till he fell unconscious on the ground. Someone reported the matter to the monastery. The monks ran to the spot and found their brother lying there. Four or five of them carried him back and laid him on a bed. He was still unconscious. The other monks sat around him sad at heart; some were fanning him. Finally someone suggested that he should be given a little milk to drink. When it was poured into his mouth he regained consciousness. He opened his eyes and looked around. One of the monks said, “Let us see whether he is fully conscious and can recognise us.” Shouting into his ear, he said, “Revered sir, who is giving you milk?” “Brother,” replied the holy man in a low voice, “he who beat me is now giving me milk.” (155)

ILLUSORY ALIKE!

THERE was a wood-cutter who was highly spiritual. One day he was dreaming a happy dream; but being suddenly awakened by some one, he exclaimed with annoyance: “Why did you awaken me? I was a king and the father of seven children. My children were all receiving education in various sciences. I was seated on the throne and ruling over my country. Why did you destroy so happy and delightful a state?" The man replied: "Oh! It was only a dream. What does it matter? The wood-cutter said: "Get away, you fool! You do not understand that my being a king was as real as my wood-cutting. If it be true that I am a wood-cutter, then it is equally true that I was a king."

According to Vedanta the waking state is no more real than the dream state. (156)

CHILDLIKE SHOULD BE THE MAN OF HIGHEST WISDOM

ONCE a sannyasini came to the royal court of Janaka. To her the king bowed, without looking at her face. Seeing this, the sannyasini said: "How strange it is, O Janaka, that you have still so much fear of woman!"

When one attains to full jnana, one's nature becomes like that of a little child—one sees no distinction between male and female. (157)

SHE BEHAVED IN A QUEER WAY

A CERTAIN devout lady, who was also a devoted wife, lived in the household serving her husband and children with a loving heart and at the same time keeping her mind fixed on the Lord. At her husband's death, as soon as the cremation was over, she broke her glass bangles and wore a pair of gold bracelets in their place. People wondered at her unnatural conduct, but she explained to them, "Hitherto my husband's body had been fragile like the glass bangles. That ephemeral body is gone; he is now like one unchangeable and full in every respect; his body is no longer fragile. So I have discarded the fragile glass bangles and worn ornaments of a permanent nature." (158)

ON COMPANY OF THE HOLY

IN THE Puranas we are told that when Uma, the Mother of the universe, incarnated Herself as the daughter of Himalaya, She blessed him with the vision of the various manifestations of the Omnipresent Mother. But when Giriraja (the King of mountains) asked her to show him the Brahman of the Vedas, Uma said, "O Father, if you wish to see Brahman, you must live in the company of holy men—men who have entirely given up the world." (159)

IN THAT DIVINE STATE

As long as there is the body, one should take care of it. But I find that the body is quite separate from the Self. When a man rids himself entirely of his love for 'woman and gold', then he clearly perceives that the body is one thing and the Self another. When the milk inside the coconut is all dried up, then the kernel becomes separate from the shell. You feel the kernel rattling inside when you shake the coconut. Or it's just like a sword and its sheath. The sword is one thing and the sheath is another.

Therefore I cannot speak much to the Divine Mother about the illness of the body.

Once, a long time ago, I was very ill. I was sitting in the Kali Temple. I felt like praying to the Divine Mother to cure my illness, but couldn't do so directly in my own name. I said to Her, "Mother, Hriday asks me to tell You about my illness." I could not proceed any further. At once there flashed into my mind the Museum of the Asiatic Society, and a human skeleton strung together with wire. I said to Her, "Please tighten the wire of my body like that so that I may go about singing your name and glories." (160)

THE NATURE OF A PARAMAHAMSA

AT ONE time I was staying at Kamarpukur when Shivaram[1] was four or five years old. One day he was trying to catch grass-hoppers near the pond. The leaves were moving. To stop their rustling he said to the leaves: "Hush! Hush! I want to catch a grass-hopper." Another day it was stormy. It rained hard. Shivaram was with me inside the house. There were flashes of lightning. He wanted to open the door and go out. I scolded him and stopped him, but still he peeped out now and then. When he saw the lightning, he exclaimed,

---

1. A nephew of the Master.

"There, uncle! They are striking matches again!"

The Paramahamsa is like a five year old child. He sees everything filled with consciousness. (161)

SRI SANKARA AND THE BUTCHER

SANKARACHARYA was a Brahmajnani, to be sure! But at the beginning he too had the feeling of differentiation. He didn't have the absolute faith that everything in the world is Brahman. One day as he was coming out of the Ganges after his bath, he saw an untouchable, a butcher, carrying a load of meat. Inadvertently the butcher touched his body. Sankara shouted angrily, "Hey there! How dare you touch me?" "Revered sir", said the butcher, "I have not touched you, nor have you touched me. The pure Self cannot be the body nor the five elements nor the twenty-four cosmic principles." Then Sankara came to his senses. (162)

Guru

(TEACHER OF MEN)

THE PHYSICIAN WITH HIS JARS OF MOLASSES

A physician prescribed medicine for a patient and said to him, "Come another day and I'll give you directions about diet." The physician had several jars of molasses in his room that day. The patient lived very far away. He visited the physician later and the physician said to him, "Be careful about your food. It is not good for you to eat molasses." After the patient left, another person who was there said to the physician, "Why did you give him all the trouble of coming here again? You could very well have given him the instruction the first day." The physician replied with a smile: "There is a reason. I had several jars of molasses in my room that day. If I had asked the patient then to give up molasses, he would not have had faith in my words. He would have thought: 'He has so many jars of molasses in his room, he must eat some of it. Then molasses can't be so bad.' Today I have hidden the jars. Now he will have faith in my words."

Renunciation of the world is needful for those whom God wants to be teachers of men. One who is an *acharya* should give up 'woman and gold'; otherwise people will not take his advice. It is not enough for him to renounce only mentally; he should also renounce outwardly. Only then will his teaching bear fruit. Otherwise people will think, "Though he asks us to give up 'woman and gold', he enjoys them himself in secret." (163)

THAT INSIGNIA OF AUTHORITY

AT Kamarpukur there is a small lake called the Haldarpukur. Certain people used to befoul its banks every day. Others who came there in the morning to bathe would abuse the offenders loudly. But the next morning they would find the same thing. The nuisance didn't stop. The villagers finally informed the authorities about it. A constable was sent, who put up a notice on the bank which read: 'Commit no nuisance.' This stopped the miscreants at once.

To teach others, one must have a badge of authority; otherwise teaching becomes a mockery. A man who is himself ignorant starts out to teach others—like the blind leading the blind! Instead of doing good, such teaching does harm. After the realisation of God one obtains an inner vision. Only then can one diagnose a person's spiritual malady and give instruction. (164)

ONE CANNOT TEACH OTHERS WITHOUT RECEIVING COMMISSION FROM GOD

THERE is no harm in teaching others if the preacher has a commission from the Lord. Nobody can confound a preacher who teaches people after having received the command of God. Getting a ray of light from the goddess of learning, a man becomes so powerful that before him scholars seem mere earthworms.

What will a man accomplish by mere lectures without the commission from God? Once a Brahmo preacher said in the course of his sermon, 'Friends, how much I used to drink!' and so on. Hearing this the people began to whisper among themselves: 'What is this fool saying? He used to drink!' Now these words produced a very unfavourable effect. This shows that preaching cannot bring a good result unless it comes from a good man.

A high Government official from Barisal[1] once said to me, 'Sir, if you begin the work of preaching I too shall gird my loins.' I told him the story[2] of people's dirtying the bank of the Haldarpukur and of its being stopped only when a constable, armed with authority from the government, put up a notice prohibiting it.

So I say, a worthless man may talk his head off preaching, and yet he will produce no effect. But people will listen to him if he is armed with a badge of authority from God.

1. A district in Bengal
2. Reference is to the tale, 'That Insignia of Authority'.

One cannot teach others without the commission from God. A teacher of men must have great power. There's many a Hanumanpuri[1] in Calcutta. It is with them that you will have to wrestle. (165)

THE AVADHUTA AND HIS UPA-GURUS

THE Guru is only one, but Upa-gurus (secondary gurus) may be many. He is an Upa-guru from whom anything whatsoever is learned. It is mentioned in the *Bhagavata* that the great *Avadhuta* (a great yogi) had twenty-four such Upa-Gurus.

(a) One day as the *Avadhuta* was walking across a meadow, he saw a bridal procession coming toward him with loud beating of drums and great pomp. Hard by he saw a hunter deeply absorbed in aiming at his game and perfectly inattentive to the noise and pomp of the procession, casting not even a passing look at it. The *Avadhuta,* saluting the hunter, said, "Sir, thou art my Guru. When I sit in meditation let my mind be concentrated upon the

1. A noted wrestler of the time,

object of meditation, as yours was on your game."

(b) An angler was fishing in a pond. The Avadhuta approaching him asked, "Brother which way leads to such and such a place?" The float of the rod at that time was indicating that the fish was nibbling at the bait; so the man did not give any reply but was all attention to his fishing rod. Having first hooked the fish, he turned round and said, "What is it you have been saying, sir?" The *Avadhuta* saluted him and said, "Sir, thou art my Guru. When I sit in contemplation of the Deity of my choice (Ishta), let me follow thy example and before finishing my devotions let me not attend to anything else."

(c) A kite with a fish in its beak was followed by a host of crows and other kites, which were pecking at it and trying to snatch the fish away. In whatever direction it went, its tormentors followed it cawing, till at last they made it let go the fish in vexation. Another kite instantly caught the fish and was in its turn followed by the whole lot. The first kite was left unmolested and sat calmly on the branch of a tree. Seeing this quiet and tranquil state of the bird the *Avadhuta,* saluting him, said, "Thou art my Guru, for thou hast taught me that peace of mind is possible in this world, only when one has given up one's adjuncts (upadhis); otherwise there is danger at every step."

(d) A heron was slowly walking on a marsh to catch a fish. Behind, there was fowler aiming an arrow at the heron, but the bird was totally unmindful of this fact. The *Avadhuta* saluting the heron, said, "When I sit in meditation, let me follow thy example and never turn back to see who is behind me."

(e) The Avadhuta found another Guru in a bee. The bee had been storing up honey with long and great labour. A man came from somewhere, broke the hive and drank up the honey. The bee was not destined to enjoy the fruit of its long labour. On seeing this, the *Avadhuta* saluted the bee saying, "Lord! Thou art my Guru; from Thee I learn what is the sure fate of accumulated riches." (166)

THE GRASS-EATING TIGER

ONCE a tigress attacked a flock of goats. As she sprang on her prey, she gave birth to a cub and died. The cub grew up in the company of the goats. The goats ate grass and cub followed their example. They bleated; the cub bleated too. Gradually it grew to be a big tiger. One day another tiger attacked the same flock. It was amazed to see the grass-eating tiger. Running after it, the wild tiger at last seized it, whereupon the grass-eating tiger began to bleat. The wild tiger dragged it to the water and said: "Look at your face in the water. It is just like mine. Here is a little meat. Eat it." Saying this, it thrust some meat into its mouth. But the grass-eating tiger would not swallow it and began to bleat again. Gradually, however, it got the taste for blood and came to relish the meat. Then the wild tiger said: "Now you see, there is no difference between you and me. Come along and follow me into the forest."

So there can be no fear if the guru's grace descends on one. He will let you know who you are and what your real nature is. (167)

HOW SRI CHAITANYA ATTRACTED THE WORLDLY

WORLDLY people will never listen to you if you ask them to renounce everything and devote themselves whole-heartedly to God. Therefore Chaitanya and Nitai, after some deliberation, made an arrangement to attract the worldly. They would say to such persons, "Come, repeat the name of Hari, and you shall have a delicious soup of magur fish and the embrace of a young woman." Many people, attracted by the fish and woman, would chant the name of God. After tasting a little of the nectar of God's hallowed name, they would soon realize that the 'fish soup' really meant the tears they shed for love of God, while the 'young woman' signified the earth. The embrace of the woman meant rolling on the ground in the rapture of divine love. (168)

LIKE TEACHER, LIKE DISCIPLE

I HAVE seen the acharya of the Adi Brahmo Samaj. I understand that he has married for the second or third time. He has grownup children. And such men are teachers! If they say, 'God is real and all else is illusory', who will believe them? You can very well understand who will be their disciples.

Like teacher, like disciple. Even if a sannyasi renounces 'Woman and Gold' mentally, but lives with them outwardly, he cannot be a teacher of men. People will say that he enjoys 'molasses'[1] secretly.

Once Mahendra Kaviraj of Sinthi gave five rupees to Ramlal. I didn't know about it. When Ramlal told me about the money, I asked him, 'For whom was the money given?' He said it was for me. At first I thought that I should use it to pay what I owed for my milk. But will you believe me? I had slept only a little while when I suddenly woke up writhing with pain, as if a cat were scratching my chest. I went to Ramlal and asked him again, 'Was the money given for your aunt?[2]' 'No', Ramlal

---

1. Reference is to the parable, 'The Physician with His jars of Molasses.'

2. The Holy Mother, his wife.

answered. Thereupon I said to him, 'Go at once and return the money.' Ramlal gave it back the next day. (169)

WHEN ALL CONCEPTIONS OF DIFFERENCES VANISH

SUKADEVA went to Janaka for instruction about the knowledge of Brahman. Janaka said to him: "You must pay me the guru's fee beforehand. When you attain the knowledge of Brahman you won't pay me the fee, because the knower of Brahman sees no difference between the guru and the disciple." (170)

Book the Fourth

Imperatives

GO FORWARD!

Once upon a time a wood-cutter went into a forest to chop wood. There suddenly he met a brahmachari. The holy man said to him, "My good man, go forward." On returning home the wood-cutter asked himself, "Why did the brahmachari tell me to go forward?" Some time passed. One day he remembered the brahmachari's words. He said to himself, "Today I shall go deeper into the forest." Going deep into the forest, he discovered innumerable sandal-wood trees. He was very happy and returned with cart-loads of sandalwood. He sold them in the market and became very rich.

A few days later he again remembered the words of the holy man to go forward. He went deeper into the forest and discovered a silvermine near a river. This was even beyond his dreams. He dug out silver from the mine and sold it in the market. He got so much money that he didn't even know how much he had.

A few days more passed. One day he thought: "The brahmachari didn't ask me to stop at the silver-mine; he told me to go forward." This time he went to the other side of the river and found a gold-mine. Then he exclaimed: "Ah, just see! This is why he asked me to go forward!"

Again, a few days afterwards, he went still deeper into the forest and found heaps of diamonds and other precious gems. He took these also and became as rich as the god of wealth himself.

Whatever you may do, you will find better and better things if only you go forward. You may feel a little ecstasy as the result of japa, but don't conclude from this that you have achieved everything in spiritual life. Work is by no means the goal of life. Go forward, and then you will be able to perform unselfish work. (171)

COUNT NOT LEAVES, EAT MANGOES

TWO friends went into an orchard. One of them possessing much worldly wisdom, immediately began to count the mango trees there and the number of leaves and mangoes each tree bore, to estimate what might be the approximate value of the whole orchard. His companion however went to the owner, made friends with him, and then, quietly going to a tree, began, at his host's desire, to pluck the fruits and eat them. Whom do you consider to be the wiser of the two? Eat mangoes! It will satisfy your hunger. What is the good of counting the trees and leaves and making calculations?

The vain man of intellect busies himself uselessly with finding out the 'why' and 'wherefore' of creation, while the humble man of wisdom makes friends with the Creator and enjoys His gift of supreme bliss. (172)

BE DROWNED!

ONCE I said to Narendra, "Look here, my boy. God is the ocean of Bliss. Don't you want to plunge into this ocean? Suppose there is a cup of syrup and you are a fly. Where will you sit to sip the syrup?" Narendra said, "I will sit on the edge of the cup and stick my head out to drink it." "Why," said I, "why should you sit on the edge?" He replied, "If I go far into the syrup, I shall be drowned and lose my life." Then I said to him: "But my child, there is no such fear in the Ocean of Satchidananda. It is the Ocean of Immortality. By plunging into It a man does not die; he becomes immortal. Man does not lose his consciousness by being mad about God." (173)

STICK TO YOUR OWN RELIGION

ONCE upon a time a man wanted to sink a well and someone advised him to dig in a certain spot, and he did so. But after sinking fifteen cubits, when he found no water coming out, he got disgusted. In the meantime another man came and laughing at his foolish attempt advised him to dig in another spot which he knew to be the best. So the man went and resumed his labour there. This time he went down twenty cubits, but no water was found.

A third man came and asked him to try in another and better place which he would point out to him. He followed and a certain spot was shown to him. He went on sinking and sinking till thirty cubits were reached and in utter disgust he was going to give up the task, when a fourth man came up to him, smiling sweetly, and said, “My child, you have laboured much indeed, but being misdirected all these labours have been of no use to you. Very well, kindly follow me, and I will take you to a spot where if you only touch your spade to the ground, water will flow out in torrents.” The temptation was too much for him and so he followed this fourth man and did according to his advice. He went on digging expecting every moment the gushing out of water, till he patiently sank twenty cubits, but alas! no water came. Then utterly discouraged he gave up the task altogether. By this time he had sunk eighty-five cubits. But if he had the patience and perseverance to sink half the number of cubits in one place, he would surely have been successful.

Similarly, men who cannot stick to their religion, and always hastily court one religion after another, at last turn out to be atheists in their old age, giving up religion altogether.

HAVE BOTH YOUR HANDS FREE

ONCE a woman went to see her weaver friend. The weaver, who had been spinning different kinds of silk thread, was very happy to see her friend and said to her: "Friend, I can't tell you how happy I am to see you. Let me get you some refreshments." She left the room. The woman looked at the threads of different colours and was tempted. She hid a bundle of thread under one arm. The weaver returned presently with the refreshments, and began to feed her guest with great enthusiasm. But, looking at the thread, she realised that her friend had taken a bundle. Hitting upon a plan to get it back, she said, "Friend, it is so long since I have seen you. This is a day of great joy for me. I feel very much like asking you to dance with me." The friend said, "Sister, I am feeling very happy too." So the two friends began to dance together. When the weaver saw that her friend danced without raising her hands, she said, "Friend let us dance with both hands raised. This is a day of great joy." But the guest pressed one arm to her side and danced raising only the other. The weaver said, "How is this, friend? Why should you dance with only one hand raised? Dance with me raising both hands. Look at me. See how I dance with both hands raised." But the guest still pressed one arm to her side. She danced with the other hand raised and said with a smile, 'This is all I know of dancing!'

Don't press your arm to your side. Have both your hands free. Be not afraid of anything. Accept both the Nitya and the Lila, both the Absolute and the Relative. (175)

LET NOT THE BELL OF BIGOTRY DEADEN YOUR HEARING

BE not a bigot like Ghantakarna.

There was a man who worshipped Siva but hated all the other deities. One day Siva appeared to him and said, "I shall never be pleased with you so long as you hate other gods." But the man was inexorable. After a few days Siva again appeared to him. This time He appeared as Hari-Hara—a form, of which one half was Siva and the other Vishnu. At this the man was half-pleased and half-displeased. He laid offerings on the side representing Siva, but nothing on that representing Vishnu. When he offered the burning incense to Siva, his beloved form of the Deity, he was audacious enough to press the nostrils of Vishnu lest he should inhale the fragrance. Then Siva said: "Your bigotry is ineradicable. By assuming this dual aspect I tried to convince you that all gods and goddesses are but the various aspects of the One Being. You have not taken the lesson in good part, and you will have to suffer for your bigotry. Long must you suffer for this." The man went away and retired to a village. He soon developed into a great hater of Vishnu. On coming to know this peculiarity of his, the children of the village began to tease him by uttering the name of Vishnu within his hearing. Vexed by this, the man hung two bells on his ears, and when the boys cried out, "Vishnu, Vishnu", he would ring the bells violently and make those names inaudible to his ears. And thus he came to be known by the name of Ghantakarna or the Bell-eared. (176)

SEE ADVAITA EVERYWHERE OR SEE IT NOWHERE

A RAJA was once taught by his Guru the sacred doctrine of Advaita, which declares that the whole universe is Brahman. The king was very much pleased with this doctrine. Going in, he said to his queen: "There is no distinction between the queen and the queen's maid-servant. So the maid-servant shall be my queen henceforth." The queen was thunder-struck at this mad proposal of her lord. She sent for the Guru and complained to him in a piteous tone, "Sir, look at the pernicious result of your teachings," and told him what had occurred. The Guru consoled the queen and said, "When you serve dinner to the king to-day, have a potful of cow-dung also served along with the dish of rice." At dinner time the Guru and the king sat down together to eat.

Who could imagine the rage of the king when he saw a dish of cow-dung served for his meal. The Guru, seeing this, calmly interrogated: "Your Highness, you are well-versed in the knowledge of Advaita. Why do you then see any distinction between the dung and the rice?" The king became exasperated and exclaimed, "You who pride yourself to be such a great Advaitin, eat this dung if you can." The Guru said, "Very well," and at once changed himself to a swine and devoured the cow-dung with great gusto and afterwards again assumed his human shape. The king became so ashamed that he never made again his mad proposal to the queen. (177)

GO BEYOND KNOWLEDGE AND IGNORANCE

Go beyond knowledge and ignorance; only then can you relize God.

To know many things is ignorance. Pride of scholarship is also ignorance. The unwavering conviction that God alone dwells in all beings is Jnana, knowledge. To know him intimately is Vijnana, a richer knowledge. If a thorn gets into your foot, a second thorn is needed to take it out. When it is out both thorns are thrown away. You have to procure the thorn of knowledge to remove the thorn of ignorance; then you must set aside both knowledge and ignorance. God is beyond both knowledge and ignorance.

Once Lakshmana said to Rama, "Brother, how amazing it is that such a wise man as Vasishtha wept bitterly at the death of his son!" Rama said, "Brother, he who has knowledge must also have ignorance. He who has knowledge of one thing must also have knowledge of many things. He who is aware of light is also aware of darkness.

Brahman is beyond knowledge and ignorance, virtue and vice, merit and demerit, cleanliness and uncleanliness. (178)

BEWARE OF THE TOUCH OF THE WORLDLINGS

(With regard to the priestly class, Sri Ramakrishna used to tell an incident from the life of Gauranga.)

WHEN Sri Gauranga, being wholly absorbed in Bhava-Samadhi, fell into the ocean. He was hauled up in a net by fisherman; but as they came into contact with his sacred person through the net they too were thrown into a trance. Abandoning all their work, they roamed about like maniacs simply chanting the sacred name of Hari. Their relatives could not cure the malady by any means, and finding no other remedy, they came at last to Sri Gauranga and told him about their sorrow. Sri Gauranga then said to them, "Get some rice from a priest's house and put it into their mouth and you will see them cured." They did accordingly and the fishermen lost their blissful ecstasy.

Such is the contaminating influence of worldliness and impurity on spiritual growth. (179)

DON'T MEASURE SPIRITUAL VALUES BY SECULAR STANDARDS

ONCE a sage was lying by the roadside deeply immersed in Samadhi. A thief while passing by that way, saw him and thought: "This fellow here must be a thief. He must have broken into some houses last night, and is now sleeping through exhaustion. The police will be very soon here to catch him. So let me escape in time." Thus cogitating he ran away. Soon after, a drunkard came there, and seeing the sage, said: "Halloa! you have fallen into the ditch by drinking too much. Eh! I am steadier than yourself and am not going to tumble down." Last of all there came a sage, and realising that a great saint was lying in the state of Samadhi, sat down by his side and began to stroke his holy feet gently.

Thus our worldly tendencies prevent us from recognising true holiness and piety.

(180)

BE WATCHFUL

ONE should be extremely watchful. Even clothes create vanity. I notice that even a man suffering from an enlarged spleen sings Nidhu Babu's light songs when he is dressed up in black-bordered cloth. There are men who spout English whenever they put on high boots.

And when an unfit person puts on an ochre cloth he becomes vain; the slightest sign of indifference to him arouses his anger and pique. (181)

GIVE THE DOG A GOOD BEATING AT TIMES

THERE was a man who had a pet dog. He used to caress it, carry it about in his arms, play with it and kiss it. A wise man, seeing this foolish behaviour of his, warned him not to lavish such affection on a dog. For it was, after all, an irrational brute, and might bite him one day. The owner took the warning to heart and putting the dog away from his arms, resolved never again to fondle it or to caress it. But the animal could not first understand the change in his master, and would run to him frequently to be taken up and caressed. Beaten several times, the dog at last ceased to trouble his master any more.

Such indeed is everybody's condition. The dog you have been cherishing (i.e., lust) so long in your bosom will not easily leave you, though you may wish to be rid of it. However, there is no harm in it. Do not caress the dog any more, but give it a good beating whenever it approaches you to be fondled, and in course of time you will be altogether free from its importunities. (182)

SINK NOW AND THEN

THE farther you advance,the more you will see that there are other things, even beyond the sandal-wood forest—mines of silver, gold and precious gems.[1] Therefore go forward.

But how can I ask people to go forward? If worldly people go too far, then the bottom will drop out of their world. One day Keshab[2] was conducting a religious service. He said, "O God, may we all sink and disappear in the river of bhakti!" When the worship was over I said to him: "Look here. How can you disappear altogether in the river of bhakti? If you do, what will happen to those seated behind the screen?[3] But do one thing: sink

1. Reference is to the parable 'Go Forward!'

2. The celebrated Brahmo leader, Keshab Chandra Sen.

3. The master referred to the ladies.

now and then, and come back again to dry land." (183)

KEEP A PART OF THE RIDGE OPEN

'WOMAN and gold' alone is the world. Many people regard money as their very life-blood. But however much you may show love for money, one day, perhaps, every bit of it will slip from your hand.

In our part[1] of the country the farmers make ridges around their paddy-fields. You know what those ridges are. Some farmers make ridges with great care all the way around their fields. Such ridges are destroyed by the rush of rain water. But some farmers leave a part of the ridge open and put sod there. The water flows through the sod, leaving the field covered with silt after the rain. They reap a rich harvest.

They alone make good use of money who spend it for the worship of God or the service of holy men and devotees. Their money bears fruit. (184)

1. Kamarpukur, a village in Bengal where Sri Ramakrishna was born.

COUNT NOT ON THE UNKNOWN FUTURE

ONCE in the month of June a kid was playing near its mother. With a merry frisk it told her that it intended to make a good feast of Ras-flowers (a species of flowers budding abundantly during the festival of Rasalila in November). "Well, my darling," replied the dam, "It is not such an easy thing as you seem to think. You will have to pass through many a danger before you can hope to feast on Ras-flowers. The ensuing months of September and October are not very auspicious to you! For some one may take you to be sacrificed to the Goddess Durga. Then there is the terrible time of Kali-puja; and if you are fortunate enough to survive that period also, there is still the Jagaddhatripuja when almost all that remain of the male members of our species are sacrificed. If your good luck carries you safely through all these crisis, then you can hope to make a feast of Ras-flowers in the beginning of November."

Like the dam in the fable, we should not hastily approve of all the aspirations which our youthful fancies may entertain, considering the manifold crisis which we may have to pass through in our lives. (185)

DISCRIMINATE EVEN IN GIVING IN CHARITY

ONCE a butcher was taking a cow to a distant slaughter-house. Being ill-treated by the butcher, the cow got unruly on the way, and the man found it very difficult to drive her.

After several hours, he reached a village at noon, and being thoroughly exhausted, he went to an alms-house nearby and partook of the food freely distributed there. Feeling himself quite refreshed after a full meal, the butcher was able to lead the cow easily to the destination.

Now, a part of the sin of killing that cow fell to the donor of the food distributed at the alms-house.

So even in giving food and alms in charity, one should discriminate and see that the recipient is not a vicious and sinning person likely to use the gift for evil purposes.

(186)

HISS YOU MAY, BUT BITE YOU SHALL NOT

SOME cowherd boys used to tend their cows in a meadow where a terrible poisonous snake lived. Everyone was on the alert for fear of it. One day a brahmachari was going along the meadow. The boys ran to him and said: "Revered sir, please don't go that way. A venomous snake lives over there." "What of it, my good children?" said the brahmachari, "I am not afraid of the snake. I know some *mantras*." So saying, he continued on his way along the meadow. But the cowherd boys, being afraid, did not accompany him. In the meantime the snake moved swiftly towards him with upraised hood. As soon as it came near, he recited a *mantra*, and the snake lay at his feet like an earthworm. The brahmachari said: "Look here. Why do you go about doing harm? Come, I will give you a holy word. By repeating it you will learn to love God. Ultimately you will realize Him and also get rid of your violent nature." Saying this, he taught the snake a holy word and initiated it into spiritual life. The snake bowed before the teacher and said, "Revered sir, how shall I practise spiritual discipline?" "Repeat that sacred word", said the teacher, "and do no harm to anybody." As he was about to depart, the brahmachari said, "I shall see you again."

Some days passed and the cowherd boys noticed that the snake would not bite. They threw stones at it. Still it showed no anger; it behaved as if it were an earthworm. One day one of the boys came close to it, caught it by the tail, and whirling it round and round, dashed it again and again on the ground and threw it away. The snake vomitted blood and became unconscious. It was stunned. It could not move. So, thinking it dead, the boys went their way.

Late at night the snake regained consciousness. Slowly and with great difficulty it dragged itself into its hole; its bones were broken and it could scarcely move. Many days passed. The snake became a mere skeleton covered with skin. Now and then, at night, it would come out in search of food. For fear of the boys it would not leave its hole during the day time. Since receiving the sacred word from the teacher, it had given up doing harm to others. It maintained its life on dirt, leaves, or the fruit that dropped from trees.

About a year later the brahmachari came that way again and asked after the snake. The cowherd boys told him that it was dead. But he couldn't believe them. He knew that the snake would not die before attaining the fruit of the holy word with which it had been initiated.

He found his way to the place and searching here and there, called it by the name he had given it.

Hearing the Guru's voice, it came out of its hole and bowed before him with great reverence. "How are you?" asked the brahmachari. "I am well, sir", replied the snake. "But", the teacher asked, "why are you so thin?" The snake replied, "Revered sir, you ordered me not to harm anybody. So I have been living only on leaves and fruit. Perhaps that has made me thinner."

The snake had developed the quality of sattva; it could not be angry with anyone. It had totally forgotten that the cowherd boys had almost killed it.

The brahmachari said: "It can't be mere want of food that has reduced you to this state. There must be some other reason. Think a little." Then the snake remembered that the boys had dashed it against the ground. It said: "Yes, revered sir, now I remember. The boys one day dashed me violently against the ground. They are ignorant, after all. They didn't realise what a great change had come over my mind. How could they know I wouldn't bite or harm anyone?" The brahmachari exclaimed: "What a shame! You are such a fool! you don't know how to protect yourself. I asked you not to bite, but I didn't forbid you to hiss. Why didn't you scare them away by hissing?"

So you must hiss at wicked people. You must frighten them lest they should do you harm. But never inject your venom into them. One must not injure others. (187)

IF YOU MUST SERVE, SERVE BUT ONE MASTER

SERVE him whom you are already serving. The mind becomes soiled by serving but one master. And to serve five masters!

Once a woman became attached to a Mussalman and invited him to her room. But he was a righteous person; he said to her that he wanted to use the toilet and must go home to get his water-jar for water. The woman offered him her own, but he said: "No, that will not do. I shall use the jar to which I have already exposed myself. I cannot expose myself before a new one." With these words he went away. That brought the woman to her senses. She understood that a new water jar, in her case, signified a paramour. (188)

FIRST CLEANSE THEE PURE, THEN PREACH AND CURE

THERE lived in a village a young man named Padmalochan. People used to call him, 'Podo' for short. In this village there was a temple in a very dilapidated condition. It contained no image of God. Aswattha and other plants sprang up on the ruins of its walls. Bats lived inside, and the floor was covered with dust and the droppings of the bats. The people of the village had stopped visiting the temple. One day after dusk the villagers heard the sound of a conchshell from the direction of the temple. They thought perhaps someone had installed an image in the shrine and was performing the evening worship. One of them softly opened the door and saw Padmalochan standing in a corner, blowing the conch. No image had been set up. The temple hadn't been swept or washed. And filth and dirt lay everywhere. Then he shouted to Podo:

> You have set no image here
> Within the Shrine, O fool!
> Blowing the conch, you simply make
> Confusion worse confounded.
> Day and night eleven bats
> Scream there incessantly.....

There is no use making a noise if you want to establish the Deity in the shrine of your heart, if you want to realize God. First of all purify the mind. In the pure heart God takes His seat. One cannot bring the holy image into the temple if the droppings of bats are all around. The eleven bats are our eleven organs: five of action, five of perception, and the mind.

First of all invoke the Deity, and then give lectures to your heart's content. First of all dive deep, plunge to the bottom and gather up the gems. Then you may do other things. (189)

EITHER 'I' ADINFINITUM OR NONE OF IT

SANKARACHARYA had a certain disciple, who served him long without receiving any teaching. One day, hearing footsteps behind him he asked, "Who is there?" and was answered by this disciple, "It is I." Then said the Master, "If this 'I' is so dear to thee, either stretch it to the infinite or renounce it altogether." (190)

Counsels

IF YOU WOULD ENJOY THE FUN!

When a man attains the knowledge of Brahman he clearly feels and sees that it is God Who has become everything. He has nothing to give up and nothing to accept. It is impossible for him to be angry with anyone.

One day I was riding a carriage. I saw two prostitutes standing on a verandah. They appeared to me to be embodiments of the Divine Mother Herself. I saluted them.

When I first attained this exalted state, I could not worship Mother Kali or give Her the food-offering. Haladhari and Hriday told me that on account of this the temple officer had slandered me. But I only laughed; I wasn't in the least angry.

A holy man came to a town and went about seeing the sights. He met another sadhu, an acquaintance. The latter said: "I see you are gadding about. Where is your baggage? I hope no thief has stolen it." The first sadhu said: "Not at all. First I found a lodging, put my things in the room in proper order, and locked the door. Now I am enjoying the fun of the city."

Attain Brahmajnana and then roam about enjoying God's lila. (191)

WHAT TO PRAY FOR?

WHILE praying to God, ask only for love for His Lotus Feet.

When Rama redeemed Ahalya[1] from the curse, He said to her, "Ask a boon of Me." Ahalya said, "O Rama, if you design to grant me a boon, then please fulfil my desire that I may always meditate on your Lotus Feet, even though I may be born in a pig's body."

I prayed to the Divine Mother only for love. I offered flowers at Her Lotus Feet and said with folded hands: "O Mother, here is Thy ignorance and here is Thy Knowledge; take them both and give me pure love for

1. See the parable 'Who can Tell' (150).

Thee. Here is Thy holiness and here is Thy unholiness; take them both and give me pure love for Thee. Here is Thy virtue and here is Thy sin; here is Thy good and here is Thy evil; take them both and give me pure love for Thee. Here is Thy dharma and here is Thy adharma; take them both and give me love for Thee." (192)

HOW TO ESCAPE PRĀRABDHA

QUESTIONER: "Sir, how can one escape *prārabdha,* the effect of action performed in previous births?"

Sri Ramakrishna: "No doubt a man experiences a little of the effect; but much of it is cancelled by the power of God's name. A man was born blind of an eye. This was his punishment for a certain misdeed he had committed in his past birth, and the punishment was to remain with him for six more births. He, however, took a bath in the Ganges, which gives one liberation. This meritorious action could not cure his blindness, but it saved him from his future births." (193)

THEN, WHAT'S THE WAY?

YOU may ask, "If worldly life is so difficult, then what is the way?"

The way is constant practice. At Kamarpukur I have seen the women of the carpenter families flattening rice with a husking-machine. They are always fearful of the pestle's smashing their fingers; and at the same time they go on nursing their children and bargaining with customers. They say to the customers, "Pay us what you owe before you leave." (194)

ONE WHO SEES 'ELEPHANT GOD' SHOULD HEED THE WORDS OF 'MAHUT GOD'

IN a forest there lived a holy man who had many disciples. One day he taught them to see God in all beings and knowing this, to bow low before them all. A disciple went to the forest to gather wood for the sacrificial fire. Suddenly he heard an outcry, "Get out of the way! A mad elephant is coming!" All but the disciple of the holy man took to their heels. He reasoned that the elephant was also God in another form.

Then why should he run away from it? He stood still, bowed before the animal, and began to sing its praises. The mahut of the elephant was shouting: "Run away! Run away!" But the disciple didn't move. The animal seized him with its trunk, cast him to one side, and went on its way. Hurt and bruised, the disciple lay unconscious on the ground. Hearing what had happened, his teacher and his brother disciples came to him and carried him to the hermitage. With the help of some medicine he soon regained consciousness. Some one asked him, "You knew the elephant was coming—why didn't you leave the place?" "But," he said, "our teacher has told us that God Himself has taken all these forms, of animals as well as of men. Therefore, thinking it was only the elephant God that was coming, I didn't run away." At this the teacher said: "Yes, my child, it is true that the elephant God was coming; but the mahut God forbade you to stay there. Since all are manifestations of God, why didn't you trust the mahut's words? You should have heeded the words of the mahut God."

God dwells in all beings. But you may be intimate only with good people; you must keep away from the evil-minded. God is even in the tiger; but you cannot embrace the tiger on that account! You may say, "Why run away from a tiger, which is also a manifestation of God?" The answer to that is: Those who tell you to run away are also manifestations of God—and why shouldn't you listen to them?

God undoubtedly dwells in the hearts of all—holy and unholy, righteous and unrighteous; but a man should not have dealings with the unholy, the wicked, the impure. He must not be intimate with them. With some of them he may exchange words, but with others one shouldn't go even that far. One should keep aloof from such people. (195)

"DAMN-DAMN-DAMN-DA-DAMN-DAMN!"

ONCE a barber was shaving a gentleman. The latter was cut slightly by the razor. At once he cried out, "Damn!" But the barber didn't know the meaning of the word. He put his razor and other shaving articles aside, tucked up his shirt-sleeves—it was winter—, and said: "You said 'Damn!' to me. Now you must tell me its meaning." The gentleman said, "Don't be silly. Go on with your shaving. The word doesn't mean anything in particular; but shave a little more carefully." But the barber wouldn't let him off so easily. He said, "If 'damn' means something good, then I am a 'damn', my father is a 'damn', and all my ancestors are 'damn'. But if it means something bad, then you are a 'damn', your father is a 'damn' and all your ancestors are 'damns'. They are not only 'damns', but 'damn—damn—damn—da—damn—damn."

In the midst of company, one should be careful not to offend others by indulging in talks which they cannot understand. (196)

BROOD OVER OTHER'S SINS, AND YOU SIN YOURSELF

A SANNYASIN dwelt by the side of a temple. There was the house of a harlot in front. Seeing the constant concourse of men in the prostitute's house, the sannyasin one day called her and censured her, saying: "You are a great sinner. You sin day and night. Oh, how miserable will be your lot hereafter." The poor prostitute became extremely sorry for her misdeeds, and with genuine inward repentance she prayed to God beseeching forgiveness. But as prostitution was her profession, she could not easily adopt any other means of earning her livelihood. And so, whenever her flesh sinned, she always reproached herself with greater contrition of heart and prayed to God more and more for forgiveness. The sannyasin saw that his advice had apparently produced no effect upon her, and thought, "Let me see how many persons will visit this woman in the course of her life." And from that day forward, whenever any person entered the house of the prostitute, the sannyasin counted him by putting a pebble aside, and in course of time there arose a big heap of pebbles. One day the sannyasin said to the prostitute, pointing to the heap: "Woman, don't you see this heap? Each pebble in it stands for every commission of the deadly sin you have been indulging in since I advised you last to desist from the evil course. Even now I tell you: Beware of your evil deeds!" The Poor wretch began to tremble at the sight of the accumulation of her sins, and she prayed to God shedding tears of utter helplessness, inwardly repeating, "Lord, wilt Thou not free me from the miserable life that I am leading?" The prayer was heard, and on that very day the angel of death passed by her house, and she ceased to exist in this world. By the strange will of God, the sannyasin also died on the same day. The messengers of Vishnu came down from Heaven and carried the spirit-body of the contrite prostitute to the heavenly regions, while the messengers of Yama bound the spirit of the sannyasin and carried him down to the nether world. The sannyasin, seeing the good luck of the prostitute, cried aloud: "Is this the subtle justice of God? I passed all my life in asceticism and poverty, and I am carried to hell, while that prostitute, whose life was a whole record of sin, is going to Heaven!" Hearing this, the messengers of

Vishnu said: "The decrees of God are always just; as you think, so you reap. You passed your life in external show and vanity, trying to get honour and fame; and God has given you this. Your prostitute earnestly prayed to God day and night, though her body sinned all the while. Look at the treatment which your body and her body are receiving from those below. As you never sinned with your body, they have decorated it with flowers and garlands, and are carrying it with music in a procession to consign it to the sacred river. But this prostitute's body, which had sinned is being torn to pieces at this moment by vultures and jackals. Nevertheless, she was pure in heart, and is therefore going to the regions of the pure. Your heart was always absorbed in contemplating her sins and thus became impure. You are therefore going to the regions of the impure. You were the real prostitute, and not she." (197)

Truths Profound

NOT 'THERE' BUT 'HERE'

Once a bird sat on the mast of a ship. When the ship sailed through the mouth of the Ganges into the 'black waters' of the ocean, the bird failed to notice the fact. When it finally became aware of the ocean, it left the mast and flew north in search of land. But it found no limit to the water and so returned. After resting a while it flew south. There too it found no limit to the water. Panting for breath the bird returned to the mast. Again, after resting a while, it flew east and then west. Finding no limit to the water in any direction, at last it settled down on the mast of the ship.

What a man seeks is very near him. Still he wanders about from place to place. As long as a man feels that God is 'there', he is ignorant. But he attains knowledge when he feels that God is 'here'. (198)

WHAT YOU ARE AFTER, IS WITHIN YOURSELF

A MAN wanted a smoke. He went to a neighbour's house to light his charcoal. It was the dead of night and the household was asleep. After he had knocked a great deal, some one came down to open the door. At the sight of the man he asked, "Hello! what's the matter?" The man replied, "Can't you guess? you know how fond I am of smoking. I have come here to light my charcoal". The neighbour said, "Ha! Ha! You are a fine man indeed! You took the trouble to come and do all this knocking at the door! Why, you have a lighted lantern in your hand!"

What a man seeks is very near him. Still he wanders about from place to place. (199)

HOW ONE CAN ENTER THE MANSION OF GOD

IT is on account of the ego that one is not able to see God. In front of the door of God's mansion lies the stump of Ego. One cannot enter the mansion without jumping over the stump.

There was once a man who had acquired the power to tame ghosts. One day, at his summons, a ghost appeared. The ghost said: "Now tell me what you want me to do. The moment you cannot give me any work I shall break your neck." The man had many things to accomplish and he had the ghost do them all, one by one. At last he could find nothing more for the ghost to do. "Now", said the ghost, "I am going to break your neck." "Wait a minute", said the man, "I shall return presently." He ran to his teacher and said, "Revered Sir, I am in great danger. This is my trouble." And he told his teacher his trouble and asked, "What shall I do now?" The teacher said, "Do this. Tell the ghost to straighten this kinky hair." The ghost devoted itself day and night to straightening the hair. But how could it make a kinky hair straight? The hair remained kinky.

Likewise, the ego seems to vanish this moment, but it reappears the next. Unless one renounces the ego, one does not receive the grace of God. (200)

THEN COMES THE TIME FOR ACTION

Do you know my attitude? Books and things like that only point out the way to reach God.

After finding the way, what more need is there of books and scriptures? Then comes the time for action.

A man received a letter from home informing him that certain presents were to be sent to his relatives. The names of the articles were given in the letter. As he was about to go shopping for them, he found that the letter was missing. He began anxiously to search for it, several others joining in the search. When at last the letter was discovered, his joy knew no bounds. With great eagerness he opened the letter and read it. It said that he was to buy five seers of sweets, a piece of cloth, and a few other things. Then he did not need the letter any more, for it had served its purpose. Putting it aside, he went out to buy the things. How long is such a letter necessary? As long as its contents are not known. When the contents are known, one proceeds to carry out the directions.

In the scriptures you will find the way to realise God. But after getting all the information about the path, you must begin to work. Only then can you attain your goal. (201)

PARTIAL KNOWLEDGE BREEDS NARROWNESS

FOUR blind men went out to see an elephant. One touched the leg of the elephant and said, "The elephant is like a pillar." The second touched the trunk and said, "The elephant is like a thick club." The third touched the belly and said, "The elephant is like a big jar." The fourth touched the ears and said, "The elephant is like a big winnowing basket." Thus they began to dispute hotly amongst themselves as to the shape of the elephant. A passer-by, seeing them thus quarrelling, said, "What is it you are disputing about?" They told him everything and asked him to arbitrate. The man said: "None of you has seen the elephant. The elephant is not like a pillar, its legs are like pillars. It is not like a winnowing basket, its ears are like winnowing baskets. It is not like a stout club, its trunk is like a club. The elephant is the combination of all these—legs, ears, belly, trunk and so on."

In the same manner, those who quarrel (about the nature of God) have each seen only some one aspect of the Deity. (202)

FANTACISM IS ANOTHER NAME FOR IGNORANCE

A FROG lived in a well. It had lived there for a long time. It was born and brought up there. And it was a small little frog. One day another frog that had lived in the sea came and fell into that well.

The frog of the well asked the new-comer, "Whence are you?" The frog of the sea replied, "I am from the sea." The frog of the well questioned: "The sea! How big is that?" The frog of the sea said, "It is very big." The frog of the well stretched its legs and questioned, "Ah! is your sea so big?" The frog of the sea said, "It is much bigger." The frog of the well then took a leap from one side of the well to the other, and asked, "Is it as big as this my well?" "My friend," said the frog of the sea, "how can you compare the sea with your well?" The frog of the well asserted: "No, there can never be anything bigger than my well. Indeed, nothing can be bigger than this! This fellow is a liar, he must be turned out."

Such is the case with every narrow-minded man. Sitting in his own little well, he thinks that whole world is no bigger than his well. (203)

NO SCRIPTURIST EVER VAUNTS OF HIS LEARNING

A LEARNED brahmana once went to a wise king and said, "I am well-versed, O king, in the holy scriptures. I intend to teach you the *Bhagavata*. The king, who was the wiser of the two, knew well that a man who had really studied the *Bhagavata* would seek to know his own Self rather than go to a king's court for wealth and honour.

So the king replied: "I see, O brahmana, that you yourself have not mastered that book thoroughly. I promise to make you my tutor, but first learn the scripture well." The brahmana went on his way thinking, "How foolish it is of the king to say that I have not mastered the *Bhagavata*, seeing that I have been reading the book over and over all these years." However, he went through the book carefully once more and appeared again before the king. The king told him the same thing again and sent him away. The brahmana was sorely vexed, but thought that there must be some mean-ing in the behaviour of the king.

He went home, shut himself up in his room, and applied himself more than ever to the study of the book. By and by, hidden meanings began to flash into his mind and the vanity of running after the bubbles of riches and honour, kings and courts, wealth and fame appeared to his un-clouded vision.

From that day forward he gave himself up entirely to attaining perfection by the worship of God, and never thought of returning to the king.

A few years after, the king thought of the brahmana and went to his house to see what he was doing. Seeing him, now radiant with Divine light and love, he fell upon his knees and said: "I see that you have now realised the true meaning of the scriptures.

I am ready to be your disciple if you will kindly condescend to make me one." (204)

UNFORTUNATE IT IS TO BE SEIZED BY A WATER-SNAKE

ONE day as I was passing the Panchavati[1] on my way to the pine-grove, I heard a bull frog croaking. I thought it must have been seized by a snake. After some time, as I was coming back, I could still hear its terrified croaking. I looked to see what was the matter, and found that a water-snake had seized it. The snake could neither swallow it nor give it up. So there was no end to the frog's suffering. I thought that had it been seized by a cobra it would have been silenced after three croaks at the most. As it was only a water-snake, both of them had to go through this agony.

. A man's ego is destroyed after three croaks, as it were, if he gets into the clutches of a real teacher. But if the teacher is

1. A group of sacred trees in the temple garden at Dakshineswar.

an 'unripe' one, then both the teacher and the disciple undergo endless suffering. The disciple cannot get rid either of his ego or of the shackles of the world. If a disciple falls into the clutches of an incompetent teacher, he does not attain liberation. (205)